HOMEMADE BAKING

HOMEMADE BAKING

Catherine Atkinson

Valerie Barrett

Gail Wagman

MQP

An Hachette Livre Company
First Published in Great Britain in 2006 by MQ Publications,
a division of Octopus Publishing Group Ltd
2–4 Heron Quays
London E14 4JP
www.octopusbooks.co.uk

Copyright © Octopus Publishing Group Ltd, 2006, 2008
Recipes: Catherine Atkinson, Valerie Barrett and Gail Wagman
Photography: Marie Louise Avery and Olivier Maynard
Home Economy: Valerie Barrett, Kim Morphew and Gail Wagman
Illustrations: Penny Brown

ISBN 13: 978-1-84601-003-3

9 8 7 6 5 4 3 2

This book contains the opinions and ideas of the author. It is intended to provide
helpful and informative material on the subjects addressed in this book and is sold
with the understanding that the authors and publisher are not engaged in rendering
any kind of personal professional services in this book. The authors and publisher
disclaim all responsibility for any liability, loss or risk, personal or otherwise, which
is incurred as a consequence, directly or indirectly, of the use and application of
any of the contents of this book.

IMPORTANT: Those who might be at risk from the effects of salmonella
poisoning (the elderly, pregnant women, young children and those suffering
from immune deficiency diseases) should consult their GP with any concerns
about eating raw eggs.

Printed and bound in China

Contents

Introduction

In today's busy society, it's easy to lose sight of just how simple it is to get in the kitchen and start baking. Ready-made goodies beckon to us from all sides, and while these give a quick fix, somehow they're never quite as satisfying as the delicious treats that Grandma used to make. Nothing comforts like the aroma of a freshly-baked cake, or a batch of warm chocolate chip cookies, and yet these delights don't have to be a fond childhood memory. Even a kitchen novice can easily learn the baking basics, and can be whipping up rounds of tantalizing Hot Choc and Marshmallow cupcakes or tasty Apple Streusel muffins in no time.

The benefits of homemade baking are obvious: no unpleasant additives or preservatives, only the freshest, most wholesome ingredients – and the best part, you can eat your delicacies fresh from the oven! Baking is an activity that the whole family can enjoy. Young children love to help mix the ingredients, and teenagers are sure to enjoy eating the results! It's also a fun way of ensuring that essential cooking skills can be learned by all. You will soon see that a little something can be baked for any occasion, whether a birthday celebration, a Christmas party or an old-fashioned family get-together, and that everyone will not only marvel at your skills, but also appreciate the unforgettable mouthwatering taste of traditional homemade baking.

This book demystifies all that is essential to successful baking and step-by-step photographs to take you through the different methods – whisking, creaming, straight mixing and rubbing – each method enabling you to make a long list of delicious cakes. The handy tips from professional bakers ensure that you avoid the most commonly experienced problems. There's even a troubleshooting section that provides easy ways to avoid baking nightmares. The recipes are divided into four simple categories – Cakes, Muffins, Cookies and Cupcakes, and there's a recipe to suit every palate, from the traditional to the gourmet. By following the recipes' simple step-by-step instructions, you'll see just how quick and easy it is to bake Caribbean Banana Bread, Strawberry Shortcake or Toffee Apple cookies from the comfort of your own kitchen.

Baking Techniques & Tips

Equipment

MEASURES

The success of all baking depends on the ingredients being in the correct proportions, so a set of accurate measuring spoons, weighing scales and a calibrated, easy-to-read measuring jug are all vital.

Kitchen scales can be electronic, balance-based or spring-operated. Electronic scales allow you to weigh out ingredients to the nearest gram and many have an add-and-weigh system so you can reset and weigh the second ingredient on top of the first.

Take particular care when measuring raising agents: over-fill the spoon first, then level the top with the back of a knife.

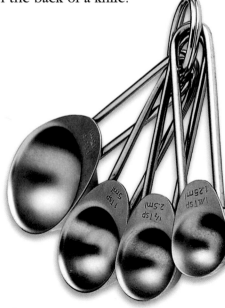

BOWLS

Whether glass, ceramic or stainless steel, a set of different-sized, heat-proof bowls for mixing, beating and melting ingredients is invaluable for baking. If possible, choose deep bowls for cake mixing rather than wide shallow ones.Small heat-proof bowls are useful for melting butter or chocolate and for beating eggs.

SIFTER

Invest in at least two strong, fine stainless-steel or plastic sieves; a larger one for sifting dry ingredients, such as flour, to remove any lumps and make it more aerated and easier to mix; and a small one for sifting icing sugar over the tops of baked cakes.

SPATULA

A flexible plastic or rubber spatula can be used to scrape the last little bit of mixture from the bowl and for smoothing the top of cakes level before baking. It is also useful for folding in delicate ingredients, such as whisked egg whites.

WHISKS

Food processors and mixers are excellent for creaming butter and sugar together, whisking eggs and sugar to a thick foam and for beating egg whites. You should, however, always fold in dry ingredients by hand to avoid over-mixing. Hand-held electric mixers are more convenient because they allow you to control the movement around the bowl. They can also be used in a bowl over a pan of barely simmering water when making whisked sponges. Wire balloon whisks and hand-held rotary whisks are good, but more time-consuming.

CAKE TINS

These are available in all sorts of shapes and sizes, from round and square tins and rectangular loaf pans to petal-, heart- and novelty-shaped ones. Look for tins made from heavy-gauge metal; the thicker the gauge, the less likely they are to warp or have hot spots. Aluminium is inexpensive, simple to clean and responds well to changes in heat. It does, however, dent easily, so treat it carefully, or, if you can afford it, choose anodized aluminium. Tin is also a good metal for bakeware, but it will rust unless thoroughly dried after use.

Non-stick tins are excellent and make turning out cakes much easier; again, they need careful use and storage, as they scratch easily. If you use tins with a dark non-stick lining, you may need to reduce the oven temperature slightly, as dark colours absorb heat.

Loose-bottomed tins simplify turning out cakes. You can also buy springform cake tins, which open out, so that the sides of the tin can simply be lifted off the cake and base. They are invaluable for delicate cakes, which should not normally be inverted after baking.

MUFFIN TINS

If you're a keen muffin-maker, it's worth buying a heavyweight muffin tin that will absorb and hold heat, helping your muffins to rise higher and have a better colour. A non-stick one is preferable, as some types of muffin are better made directly in the tin rather than in paper cases. A standard muffin tin has 12 cups, each about 7cm in diameter and 3cm deep.

Mini muffin tins are also popular; again, they have 12 cups, but these are a dainty 4cm in diameter and 2cm deep.

The new non-stick silicone muffin moulds can be used at high temperatures without any additional preparation. They are extremely easy to clean and in some types the material bends, allowing the muffins to pop out easily. You do, however, need to place a baking sheet under the non-rigid ones.

CUPCAKE TINS

Cupcake tins come in a variety of sizes, but the three major sizes are 'mini' (3–5cm in diameter, holding 30ml or 2 tablespoons of batter), 'regular' (7cm in diameter, holding 60 to 80ml of batter) and 'jumbo' (8.5cm in diameter, holding about 150ml of batter). The number of cups in the tin is variable, either 20 or 30. There are usually 12 cups in a regular-sized cupcake tin, whereas the silicone ones are often smaller. A jumbo tin usually makes six cupcakes. Tins come in metal, in which case you have to grease and flour them if you are not using cupcake papers. Silicone cupcake moulds offer all the same advantages as silicone muffin moulds.

BAKING SHEETS

FOR CAKES

These can be used in combination with cake hoops and novelty cake tins without bases. They may be entirely flat or have a lip along the length of one side. It is vital to choose good-quality, heavy ones, which won't distort at high temperature. For cake-making, avoid baking sheets that are very dark, as they absorb more heat, which means that the base of the cake will burn more easily.

COOKIES

Cookies can burn easily, so it is wise to buy heavy, professional-quality sheets and tins. Lining with baking paper helps promote even baking, as does placing a thin baking sheet or brownie tin on top of another baking sheet for extra insulation. Baking sheets should be rimless or with low rims so that it

is easy to remove the cookies. Air-cushioned baking sheets bake evenly but they may take a little longer and are generally better when you want soft, chewy cookies rather than crisp ones.

SUGAR THERMOMETER

This is the most reliable way to check the temperature of a boiling sugar syrup when making caramel or some icings.

TIMER

This is essential, as even an extra couple of minutes in the oven can result in a dry, over-cooked cake, cookie or muffin. Most modern ovens have a timer, but a hand-held digital or rotating dial timer is useful, particularly if you want to go into another room while your goods are baking.

WIRE RACK

Whether they are turned out of their tins straight away, or left to cool partially or completely in their tins, it is best to rest baked goods on a wire rack. This allows air to circulate, so that the cake, cookies or muffins cools quickly, and prevents trapped warmth, which would make the bases soggy.

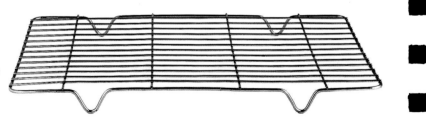

PIPING BAGS & NOZZLES

These are useful for piping whipped cream, frostings, icing and melted chocolate onto cakes, cookies and muffins. Most piping bags are now made of nylon; the best are glued and double stitched along the seams to prevent splitting or leakage. You can also buy disposable plastic piping bags.

ROLLING PIN

Cookie dough is often rolled out to quite a large size so it is preferable to have a rolling pin that is straight and without handles.

AIRTIGHT CONTAINERS

Because homemade baked goods do not contain preservatives, they should be stored in an airtight tin or plastic container as soon as they are cool to keep them fresh. Cheesecake types and those covered with butter-based icing or cream toppings, or containing ingredients such as fresh fruit, should be stored in the refrigerator.

PAPER MUFFIN & CUPCAKE CASES

You can lightly grease muffin or cupcake tins, but for ease, paper cases make a great alternative. Not only do they save time and washing up, but they also help keep muffins and cupcakes fresh and make packing or cold lunches and picnics a doddle. Plain pleated white paper cups are the most economical, but there is also a huge range of fancy designs for every occasion available.

PASTRY BRUSHES

A pastry brush gives an all-over, even finish to a sticky glaze, such as honey, maple syrup and hot sugar syrups. Choose a brush with either natural bristles fixed in a wooden handle or one with nylon bristles and a plastic handle. After use, rinse in cold water, then wash in hot soapy water, flick dry and leave to air before using again.

COOKIE CUTTERS

There are many cutters available in myriad shapes and sizes. For best results, the cutter should be sharp and have a good, clear outline. This generally means that they should be made of metal rather than plastic, but some plastic versions do have a sharp enough edge. To use a cutter, place gently on the dough and, using the palm of your hand, press firmly and evenly down on the cutter. Lift the cutter off without twisting it. Some doughs may be slightly sticky or moist, so dip the edge of the cutter in flour every now and then.

KNIVES

A large, sharp knife is good for cutting cleanly through rolled out or refrigerated cookie dough. Even more useful is a round-bladed palette knife for spreading and smoothing mixtures and icing or chocolate, transferring cut-out cookies to baking sheets and removing them once cooked.

BAKING PAPER

Non-stick baking paper is used to line baking sheets so that cookies don't stick. It's also useful for sandwiching soft or sticky dough when rolling out.

Ingredients

FLOUR

The most common variety of flour is soft wheat flour, either plain or, more often, self-raising, which has added raising agents. With a low gluten content, these flours form a soft, cake-like texture, perfect for muffins or sponges. However, when using a flour that contains gluten, it is important not to beat a mixture too much after adding the flour, as this will develop the gluten, giving the sponge a tough texture. Always use a good premium brand. These days it is rare to find lumpy flour, so sifting isn't always necessary, but it does add more air, making it easier to mix in.

SELF-RAISING FLOUR

When using self-raising flour in particular, always check the 'use-by' date, as the raising agents gradually deteriorate. Raising agents are sometimes used in addition to self-raising flour, particularly in all-in-one mixtures where less air will be beaten in. Don't be tempted to add more than the recipe states, or your sponge will rise rapidly, then sink unevenly when removed from the oven, and the taste will be adversely affected. Some supermarkets sell 'sponge flour', which is a self-raising flour finely milled from especially soft wheat.

OTHER FLOURS

Wholemeal flour is milled from the whole wheat kernel and is coarser in texture, giving a heavier result, so it is often combined with plain flour. Avoid sifting wholemeal flour, as you will be taking out all the goodness.

Cornmeal, also known as instant polenta or maizemeal, has tiny bright yellow grains and is particularly good in savoury muffins or cakes. Most recipes require medium-ground cornmeal, unless stated otherwise. Cornflour is a fine white powder made from cornmeal. Used in small quantities combined with flour, it gives a lighter, smooth texture.

Gluten-free flours include soya flour from soya beans, with a distinctive nutty taste and rice flour from white or brown rice, which results in a crumbly texture.

RAISING AGENTS

Baking powder is a mixture of cream of tartar and bicarbonate of soda, and releases carbon dioxide bubbles when it comes into contact with a liquid. If you want to substitute plain flour for self-raising in any recipe, you will need to add 1 teaspoon of baking powder for every 100g of flour.

Bicarbonate of soda needs an acid ingredient as well as liquid to be activated, such as citrus juice, buttermilk or yoghurt.

BUTTER

Out of all the baking ingredients (other than chocolate), butter has the most effect on flavour and texture, so use the best that you can afford. Salted butter will keep well in the refrigerator for up to a month; unsalted for just two weeks. However, both can be frozen for up to 6 months.

When used in creamed mixtures, butter should always be soft, but not melting (around room temperature), so that it can be successfully combined with the sugar. If a recipe requires melted butter, cut it into small pieces, so that it melts quickly, and set over a pan of water (or microwave in a bowl) barely simmering to prevent it burning. Remove it from the heat when it has almost melted and allow the residual heat to finish the job. For rubbed-in mixtures, remove the butter from the refrigerator about 10 minutes before using, so that it is still cold but not too hard.

Unsalted butter should be used to grease cake tins or muffin pans, as salted butter may make the edges stick.

OTHER FATS

'Hard' block margarine can be used as an alternative to butter in most recipes, and is less expensive, although it doesn't have the same creamy taste.

Soft-tub margarine is often used in all-in-one mixtures, as it can be used straight from the refrigerator and blends quickly and easily. However, you should avoid using low-fat margarines and spreads, as they have a high water content and will upset the balance of many recipes.

Oil is sometimes used in muffins instead of solid fat. It's especially good in quick-mix muffins because, unlike butter, it doesn't need to be melted and cooled first.

EGGS

Most of the recipes in this book use medium eggs unless stated otherwise. Always use eggs at room temperature, as cold eggs may curdle and cold egg whites will produce less volume when whisked. Farm fresh, organic or free-range eggs taste better and give a better result than battery eggs. Eggs will absorb flavours from other foods, so they should be kept in their box or a separate compartment in the refrigerator and stored pointed-end downwards, to prevent moisture in the egg evaporating.

SUGAR

There are many different types of sugar, each with its own distinct characteristics. Always use the type of sugar specified by a particular recipe.

Caster sugar has fine grains and is most commonly used for creamed mixtures, as it combines beautifully with butter, trapping lots of air. Golden caster sugar is the unrefined version and has a pale gold colour.

Granulated sugar has large granules and is mostly used for sprinkling over baked goods as a crunchy topping. Larger grain sugars are also sometimes used in rubbed-in recipes.

Demerara sugar has a deep golden colour and a toffee-like flavour.

Icing sugar is ground to a fine powder. It makes smooth icings and frostings, and may also be used as a dusting to give an easy, professional finish.

Soft light and dark brown sugar are refined white sugars that have been tossed in syrup or molasses to darken the colour and to flavour them. Soft brown sugar adds more moisture than caster sugar, so if you substitute one for the other, add a tiny bit less or more liquid to compensate.

Muscovado sugar is unrefined 'raw' cane sugar and may be light or dark. Very moist, it has fine grains and a treacly flavour, tending to be slightly less sweet than refined sugars.

Other sweeteners include golden syrup, maple syrup, honey, molasses and malt extract.

FRUIT AND NUTS

Both fresh and dried fruits can be folded into a mixture or used for decoration. Dried fruit, including apples, apricots, tropical fruits, sour cherries, cranberries and blueberries, crystallized fruit and candied citrus peel or grated zest may be added to a recipe without altering the consistency of the batter. You can usually substitute one type of dried fruit for another in a recipe. Always use good-quality, plump and moist dried fruit for the best flavour.

When fruit is dried, the flavour and sweetness is intensified, so recipes containing a large amount of dried fruit often contain less sugar to compensate.

If you want to add fresh fruit, use a specific recipe, as the additional moisture will affect the final result. Citrus rinds or zest should always be taken from unwaxed fruit, which has been washed before use.

Nuts should be as fresh as possible, as the oils they contain can turn rancid. Store opened packets in the freezer if you are not going to use them regularly. When chopping or grinding nuts in a food processor, always use a perfectly dry bowl and use the pulse button, scraping them down occasionally to avoid over-processing them to a paste.

CHOCOLATE

Chocolate is a popular flavouring. For the best flavour, it is vital to use one with a high percentage of cocoa solids – 70% or more is ideal. Some recipes call for milk or white chocolate; always look for the cooking variety and not confectionery bars.

Unsweetened cocoa powder is a dark bitter powder that can be substituted for the same quantity of flour in many recipes. Avoid using drinking chocolate, unless specified by the recipe, as it contains only about 25% cocoa powder, the remainder being sugar.

Chocolate chips or dots are a quick way to add chocolate flavour and come in milk, white and plain varieties. Unless stated in the recipe, never use chocolate chips to replace chocolate that is to be melted or blended into the mixture, as they are formulated to keep their shape when cooked and are sweeter and less smooth in texture.

ADDING FLAVOUR

Any spices used should be as fresh as possible. Only buy in small quantities, and if they don't smell wonderfully fresh when opened, then it is time to renew your supply. Warm spices, such as cinnamon and ginger, work particularly well in sweet recipes. Vanilla is probably the most frequently added spice and provides a delicate, subtle flavour. It is often used in combination with many other flavourings, including chocolate. Choose a quality, pure extract if you can, for a superior finished flavour.

Spirits, such as rum and brandy, sherry and liqueurs are sometimes used in small quantities to add flavour. They can also be used to soak dried fruit before adding it to a batter – the alcohol will evaporate during baking, leaving a subtle taste behind. Sometimes alcohol is sprinkled on the top after baking to leave a stronger flavour.

Salt helps bring out the flavour in both sweet and savoury recipes. If you prefer, you can use a low-sodium substitute.

METHODS OF CAKE-MAKING

There are as many different ways of making cakes as there are cakes to make, but they're all based on the same core technique – whisking. The method and quantities of ingredients are then subtly altered to make the cake drier, moister or lighter. Cake-making really is a fine art!

The Basic Method

The technique of whisking is essential in the making of sponge cakes. Try this traditional method to make a light, airy-textured cake.

STEP 1

Separate the eggs, put the yolks into a large, roomy mixing bowl and add sugar. Whisk together using a hand-held electric mixer until the egg yolks are thick and pale yellow.

STEP 2

Remove the beaters and wash them. In a separate bowl, with the clean beaters, start whisking the egg whites, moving the beaters all round the bowl.

STEP 3

Keep on whisking the egg whites – you can use a balloon whisk instead of the electric mixer if preferred – until they reach the stiff peak stage.

STEP 4

Gradually whisk in the sugar, sprinkling it over the surface 1 tablespoon at a time. Make sure that it is mixed well before adding the next, whisking until stiff and glossy.

STEP 5

Sift the flour over the egg yolks in the first bowl, then fold it in carefully, using a spatula or large metal spoon. Finally, carefully fold in the whisked egg whites.

Creaming

Creamed mixtures are notorious for separating, so make sure all the ingredients are at room temperature before you start, which helps. Here, butter and sugar are whipped or 'creamed' together until pale and fluffy to incorporate plenty of air. Add the eggs one at a time, getting yet more air into the cake mixture. This is the key to its success. The flour is gently folded in, which stops the cake from toughening. Proportions are generally equal weights, but this can vary slightly.

STEP 1

Whisk the butter and sugar with an electric hand-held mixer or a balloon whisk in a large mixing bowl until they are pale and fluffy, and no longer grainy.

STEP 2

Break the eggs into a separate bowl. Using a balloon whisk, whisk the eggs to break them up slightly. This makes them easier to add to the rest of the mixture.

STEP 3

A little at a time, gradually whisk the beaten eggs into the butter and sugar mixture in the first bowl. Make sure that you whisk well after each addition of egg.

STEP 4

Sift over the flour and any other dry ingredients such as ground nuts or cocoa powder. Fold into the mixture gently, with the electric mixer set at a slow speed, until combined.

3 Steps for Testing Cakes

1 The centre of the cake is the last part to be cooked, so test the centre once the cooking time is up.
2 With sponge cakes, a gentle touch of the top will tell you if the cake is cooked. If your fingertips leave no impression and the mixture springs back, the cake is done. The mixture will also have started to pull away from the sides of the tin.
3 For heavier cakes, insert a thin skewer into the centre of the cake. When removed, it should have no batter stuck to it.

All-in-one

This method means just that. All the main ingredients go into a bowl and are beaten together using a hand-held electric mixer or tabletop mixer until soft and creamy. If the butter is very soft, the ingredients can be beaten by hand, but this can be very hard work. It is important that the butter is very soft to ensure even blending and that an extra raising agent, such as baking powder, is used to compensate for the lack of air usually incorporated at the creaming stage. This method produces cakes with a slightly closer texture.

Rubbing-in

This method is used for cakes that are typically made with half, or less than half, fat to flour and gives a fairly open texture. It is often used for light fruit cakes and tea loaves. The fat is cut into small pieces, then rubbed into the flour with the fingertips until the mixture resembles fine breadcrumbs, then the remaining ingredients are stirred in.

Melting

Often used for moist cakes, such as gingerbread and fruit cake, the fat, sugar, syrup and sometimes fruit are all gently heated in a saucepan over the hob until just melted. The mixture is usually cooled before the eggs and remaining dry ingredients are stirred in. Fat should be at room temperature and cut it into small pieces so that it melts before the other ingredients are over-heated.

7 Steps to Successful Cake-making

1 Beat eggs when they are at room temperature if you want the best volume.
2 Use softened, not melted, butter for easier blending.
3 Gently tap tins on the worktop after filling to prevent air bubbles.
4 Preheat the oven properly. Ensure the oven is at the correct temperature before you put the cake in; an oven thermometer is invaluable.
5 Bake cakes in the centre of your oven. If making more than two layers, switch the position of the tins halfway through cooking.
6 Do not open the oven door during the first 15 minutes of baking or your cake may sink.
7 Unless the recipe specifies otherwise, use caster sugar; coarser sugars don't blend in with the mixture as well.

LINING TINS

Line your cake tins before preparing the mixture so the cake can go straight into the oven with no delay. Before lining, grease tins with oil or melted and cooled unsalted butter or white vegetable fat. Melted vegetable shortening is the best thing to use when greasing pans. Use a pastry brush to brush a thin layer over the inside of the tin.

Bases

Most cake recipes require only the bottom of the tin to be lined with non-stick baking or greaseproof paper. Place the tin on a double folded sheet of paper and draw around the pan with a pencil. Cut out the shape inside the pencil mark to give two rounds or squares and place both pieces in the base of the tin. Alternatively, precut bases can be bought for ease.

Sides

To line the sides of the tin, cut a double strip of greaseproof paper long enough to reach around the tin and high enough to extend 2.5cm above the top. Fold one edge of the strip over by 2.5cm, then use scissors to snip cuts at 2.5cm intervals along its length. Place the snipped edge into the base of the pan using a greased pastry brush to push the fold into the base corners. Place the round or square base on top, covering the snipped edge.

5 Steps for Storing Cakes

1 The best way to store cakes is to freeze them on the day of baking.
2 Leave the heavier cakes in their lining paper and then overwrap with cling film or seal in a freezer bag. Wrap sponge cakes in greaseproof paper, then overwrap in cling film or seal in a freezer bag.
3 For short-term storage, place cooled cakes in an airtight container.
4 Always keep cakes with fresh cream fillings in the refrigerator.
5 Fatless sponge cakes will keep for 1–2 days; other beaten sponges, 3 days; creamed mixtures, 1 week; light fruit cakes, 2 weeks; rich fruit cakes, if stored well, 2–3 months.

Troubleshooting

All the recipes in this book have foolproof, step-by-step instructions to help ensure that your baking is perfect every time. However, occasionally problems do occur, and it's important to find out what went wrong and why, so you can avoid the same mistake next time.

Q – I haven't got a tin in the right size. Is it OK to use one slightly bigger or smaller?

A – For the best results, always use the tin size recommended in your chosen recipe, as it may not bake successfully in a tin that is markedly different in size. It's not a good idea to use a smaller tin, as the mixture may overflow. Sometimes you can use a slightly larger tin, but remember to adjust the cooking time if you do so, as the mixture will be shallower and will cook much faster. If you don't have a big selection of tins, it may be worth investing in a 'multi-size' cake tin, which can be adjusted to the size you require. If you want to bake a round cake instead of a square one, or vice versa, an 18cm round is the equivalent of a 15cm square and a 23cm round the equivalent of a 20cm square.

Q – I need a cake for a special occasion in a few months' time. What sort of cake would be best to make in advance and how should I store it?

A – Sponges made with the creaming method, such as a Victoria sponge cake, can be covered with fondant icing and will keep well for up to a week if wrapped in foil and kept in a clean airtight tin or plastic container. Alternatively, you can freeze an undecorated sponge for up to a month. If you want a cake that can be made well ahead, choose a rich fruit cake. This should be made two to three months before you decorate it to allow the cake to mature; its keeping qualities will improve further if you brush the top with alcohol, such as brandy or rum. After baking the cake, make sure that it is completely cold, then wrap it in a double layer of greaseproof paper, then in foil.

Q – I'm never quite sure when to take my cake out of the oven. How can I tell whether it's properly cooked or not?

A – To test a baked sponge, press the centre gently with a fingertip; it should feel spongy and give very slightly, then rise immediately, leaving no impression. A whisked sponge should be just shrinking away from the sides of the tin. To test a fruit cake, insert a fine skewer into the centre, leave it for 5 seconds, then remove. It should come away cleanly; if any mixture is sticking to the skewer, bake it for a little longer.

Q – Whenever I make a sponge cake and add the eggs to the creamed butter and sugar mixture, it curdles. Does this matter and how can I prevent it?

A - If the creamed mixture curdles when you add the eggs, some of the air you've carefully beaten in will be lost and your cake won't rise quite as well. All the ingredients must be at room temperature before you start. If your kitchen is cold, stand the butter and sugar over a bowl of warm water for a few minutes, then place the bowl of beaten eggs over the water while you cream the butter and sugar. Add the beaten eggs a little at a time, beating thoroughly after each addition. If you see the mixture start to separate, beat in a spoonful of sifted flour before adding the rest of the eggs.

Q – My sponge cakes always look perfect when I take them out of the oven, but stick to the tin when I try to turn them out, no matter how well I grease them. What am I doing wrong?

A - It's really disheartening when you damage your cake trying to remove it from the tin. For most cakes, you will need to line the tin with non-stick baking paper – either just the base or the sides too – even if the tin is a non-stick one. If you use greaseproof paper, you may need to brush it lightly with oil or melted and cooled unsalted butter or white vegetable margarine. Once removed from the oven, whisked sponges should be turned out straight away, but all other cakes benefit from being left in the tin for a few minutes to firm up and to allow the cake to shrink slightly from the sides. Some, such as rich fruit cakes, can be left in the tin until completely cool – each recipe will give advice on this. To remove the cake, run a palette knife around the edge of the tin. Turn the cake onto a wire cooling rack covered with a clean tea towel, remove the lining paper, then cover the cake with another cooling rack. Invert both racks together and remove the top rack. Loose-bottomed cake tins make removal considerably easier, but don't use them for very wet mixtures or upside-down cakes, or some of the mixture may seep out during baking.

Q – Although they look perfect on the outside, my muffins have 'tunnels' of air in them when broken open. How can I avoid this?

A - Quite simply, you're over-mixing the batter. Tunnels are caused by an excess of air bubbles in the mixture. Excessive stirring also develops the gluten in the flour, so the muffins will be tough. Next time, gently stir the dry and wet ingredients together until they are just combined. Stop mixing while the batter is still a little lumpy.

Q – Unfortunately, I can't eat butter and would like to make muffins with oil instead. Is this possible?

A – Yes, butter and oil are interchangeable in most recipes. Remember, though, that butter contains only about 80% fat, the other 20% being milk solids and water, so reduce the amount of oil very slightly and make up to the same amount with a dash of milk or water, e.g. if a recipe calls for 8 tablespoons of butter, use 7 tablespoons of oil and 1 tablespoon of milk or water. When choosing oil, sunflower or safflower oils are preferable for sweet muffins because they have a mild flavour, while for muffins containing nuts, groundnut oil works well. The more distinctive flavour of olive oil is good for many savoury muffin recipes.

Q – Some recipes only make 9 or 10 muffins. I find my muffin tin warps when I don't fill all 12 cups with mixture, making them rise unevenly. What can I do?

A – Even good-quality, heavyweight muffin tins warp sometimes. You can prevent this happening by pouring some hot water into any empty muffin cups before baking – they should be about one-third full. The steam will help the muffins to rise as well.

Q – My last batch of muffins were dry and tough. What did I do wrong?

A – There are a couple of reasons why this may have happened. Firstly, when making muffins, the ratio of flour to liquid is vital, so always measure

these carefully. Another cause of tough, dry muffins is over-baking; they are ready as soon as the tops spring back when lightly pressed with a finger, or when a cocktail stick inserted into the centre comes out clean.

Q – My muffins are always slightly flat, even though I measure carefully and use fresh raising agents. Could my oven be at fault?

A – Temperature is one of the secrets to well-risen, domed muffins. Make sure that the oven is completely heated before you bake your muffins and close the oven door as quickly as possible to keep the heat trapped. Try setting the oven temperature slightly higher initially, then lower it as soon as you've added the muffins. This extra heat will create a burst of steam to help raise the batter.

Q – When the recipe calls for softened butter, what is this?

A – If you're using an electric mixer, the butter should be left at room temperature until it gives slightly when pressed. If you are using a wooden spoon, the butter should be the consistency of thick mayonnaise. Butter can be softened in the microwave at 30% power.

Q – The first tray of cookies I bake are always OK, but the cookies on subsequent trays are often deformed – why is this?

A - Always cool baking sheets before putting on a new batch of raw cookies. Warm sheets will start the dough melting slowly and this will cause the cookies to spread and become deformed.

Q – I always find it difficult to measure very sticky ingredients such as golden syrup. How can I make it easier?

A - To measure golden syrup and black treacle accurately, open the can or jar and rest the lid on top. Place in a bowl and fill with boiling water to halfway up the side of the can or jar. Leave for a few minutes until the syrup or treacle is runny and easy to measure accurately.

Q – I often find my dough to be very sticky and soft, so I add extra flour when rolling out, but then my cookies turn out tough. What is the solution?

A - Always refrigerate a dough rather than be tempted to add any extra flour. More flour equals a drier mixture, which will result in a tougher cookie. Alternatively, roll out the dough between sheets of non-stick baking paper.

Q – My cookies always seem to bake unevenly. Why is this?

A - Always rotate the baking sheets halfway through the baking time. If you are baking more than one sheet of cookies at a time, reverse them top to bottom and front to back. Also make sure that all the cookies are the same size. If you are unsure of your oven, fine tune the baking of cookies by test baking 3 or 4 cookies first.

Q – How can I make sure that my drop cookies are all even-sized?

A - A good trick is to use a small, round ice-cream scoop or lightly oiled measuring tablespoon.

Q – I like to make cookies and usually make the drop variety – occasionally I would like to try other types, but I don't have any cookie cutters.

A - To cut cookie dough rounds without a cutter use a sturdy inverted wine glass. Alternatively, form small amounts of the cookie dough into balls and flatten.

Q – My cookies are often tough and dry – why is this?

A - There could be a few reasons for this. Make sure that your measuring is accurate. Do not over-mix the dough once the flour has been added, as this will cause the gluten to develop and create a tough cookie. The same applies to kneading and rolling out – keep it to a minimum and do not add extra flour. If the dough is sticky, chill it for a while and roll out between sheets of non-stick baking paper. It could also be that you are leaving the cookies in the oven too long. Even a minute or two extra can make them dry and tough, so remove them just before you think they are done, as they will continue to cook for a short time.

CAKES

- Passion Cake
- Buttermilk Cake
- Fruit Tea Loaf
- Squidgy Chocolate Cake
- Sugar & Spice Cake
- Chocolate Marble Cake
- Rocky Road Cake
- Jelly Bean Swiss Roll
- Cherry Loaf Cake
- Apricot Frangipane Cake
- Lemon & Ginger Cake
- Caribbean Banana Bread
- Apple, Cranberry & Cider Cake
- Orange & Almond Sponge Cake

- Gooey Chocolate Cake
- Angel Food Cake
- Plum & Amaretti Sponge Cake
- Coconut Cream Cake
- Date & Walnut Loaf
- Apple Crumb Cake
- Pineapple Upside-Down Cake
- Gooseberry & Elderflower Cake
- Chocolate & Strawberry Layer Cake
- Coffee, Maple & Pecan Sponge Cake
- Caramel Pecan Loaf
- Hazelnut Meringue Cake
- Chocolate Refrigerator Cake

- Iced Lime Traybake
- New York Cheesecake
- Dark Chocolate Cheesecake
- Lady Baltimore Cake
- Whipped Cream Cheesecake
- Strawberry Cake with Flaked Almonds
- Fruit Gingerbread
- Golden Buttercream Cake
- Rum Cake
- Tropical Fruit Cake
- Strawberry Shortcake
- Carrot & Brazil Nut Traybake
- Valentine Cake
- Iced Sponge Cake

CHAPTER ONE

CAKES

Passion Cake

Makes 9 squares

150ml safflower or sunflower oil
175g soft light brown sugar
3 eggs, beaten
½ teaspoon ground cinnamon
½ teaspoon freshly grated nutmeg
150g carrots, coarsely grated
1 banana, peeled and mashed
50g pecan nuts, chopped
250g plain flour, sifted
1 tablespoon baking powder

For the icing
160g cream cheese or full-fat soft
   cheese
100g icing sugar, sifted
Finely grated zest of ½ orange
50g pecan nuts, chopped (optional)

1 Preheat the oven to 180°C/350°F/Gas mark 4. Grease and base line a deep 20cm square cake tin.

2 Put all the cake ingredients into a large bowl and beat together until well mixed.

3 Spoon the mixture into the prepared tin and level the surface. Bake in the oven for 45–50 minutes, or until golden and a skewer inserted into the centre comes out clean.

4 Cool in the tin for 10 minutes, then turn out onto a wire rack and leave to cool completely.

5 Meanwhile, to make the icing, beat the cream cheese or soft cheese in a bowl to soften. Add the icing sugar and orange zest and beat together until pale and fluffy. Spread the icing over the top of the cake and sprinkle with pecan nuts before serving, if you like. Cut into squares to serve.

Buttermilk Cake

Makes 18 Slices

175g unsalted butter, softened
300g caster sugar
300ml buttermilk
1 teaspoon vanilla extract
275g self-raising flour
1 teaspoon baking powder
½ teaspoon bicarbonate of soda
Pinch of salt
4 egg whites

Tip

If you can't get hold of buttermilk, use 150ml of milk mixed with 150ml of natural yoghurt.

1 Preheat the oven to 180°C/350°F/Gas mark 4. Grease and base line a 28 x 20 x 4cm cake tin or baking tin.

2 Cream the butter and sugar together in a bowl with 1 tablespoon of the buttermilk and the vanilla extract until pale and fluffy.

3 Sift the flour, baking powder, bicarbonate of soda and salt together three times into a separate bowl. Stir the flour mixture and remaining buttermilk alternately into the creamed mixture until well combined.

4 In a separate bowl, whisk the egg whites until stiff. Stir one-third of the whisked egg whites into the sponge mixture to loosen it, then gently fold in the remainder.

5 Pour the mixture evenly into the prepared tin. Bake in the oven for 35–40 minutes, or until just firm to the touch. Cool in the tin for 5 minutes, then turn out onto a wire rack and leave to cool completely. Serve in slices.

Fruit Tea Loaf

Makes 8–10 slices

300g mixed dried fruit, such as
  sultanas, currants, raisins and
  glacé cherries
125g soft light brown sugar
125g unsalted butter, cut into small
  pieces
200ml brewed tea
2 teaspoons ground allspice
Finely grated zest of 1 orange
225g self-raising flour, sifted
1 tablespoon clear honey, warmed
Softened butter, to serve (optional)

Tip
For a scented
flavour, use a tea
such as Earl or
Lady Grey.

1 Place the mixed dried fruit, sugar, butter, tea and allspice in a saucepan. Cover and heat gently until the butter has melted, stirring occasionally. Bring to the boil and boil for 1 minute, then remove the pan from the heat. Add the orange zest, then set aside to cool. Cover and leave overnight at room temperature.

2 Preheat the oven to 180°C/350°F/Gas mark 4. Grease and base line a 450g loaf tin.

3 Fold the sifted flour into the fruit mixture. Spoon the mixture into the prepared tin and level the surface. Bake in the oven for 50–55 minutes, or until golden and a skewer inserted into the centre comes out clean.

4 Remove the cake from the oven, brush the top of the cake with the warmed honey, then leave to cool completely in the tin. Turn out and serve in slices, spread with butter, if you like.

Squidgy Chocolate Cake

Makes 12–14 slices

100g gluten-free plain flour
30g rice flour
4 tablespoons unsweetened cocoa
    powder
$\frac{1}{4}$ teaspoon bicarbonate of soda
$\frac{1}{2}$ teaspoon gluten-free baking powder
115g walnuts, chopped
175g dark bitter or plain chocolate,
    broken into squares
125g dairy-free margarine
4 eggs
300g golden caster sugar
2 teaspoons vanilla extract

For the icing
125ml coconut milk
125g dark bitter or plain
    chocolate, chopped
40g dairy-free
    margarine
25g walnuts, chopped (optional)

1 Preheat the oven to 180°C/350°F/Gas mark 4. Grease and line a 23cm round loose-bottomed sandwich cake tin.

2 For the cake, sift the flour, rice flour, cocoa powder, bicarbonate of soda and baking powder into a bowl. Stir in the walnuts. Set aside.

3 Melt the chocolate and margarine together in a heat-proof bowl set over a pan of barely simmering water. Remove from the heat and set aside to cool slightly. In a separate bowl, beat the eggs, sugar and vanilla extract together. Stir in the melted chocolate mixture, then add this to the flour mixture and stir together until just combined.

4 Spoon the mixture into the prepared tin and level the surface. Bake in the oven for about 30 minutes, or until firm to the touch. Remove the cake from the oven and cool in the tin for about 20 minutes, then turn out carefully and place on a serving plate. Set aside to cool completely.

5 Meanwhile, to make the icing, put the coconut milk in a small saucepan and bring to the boil. Remove the pan from the heat and immediately add the chocolate and margarine to the hot milk. Stir well until smooth, then leave to cool until the mixture is of a thick spreading consistency. Spread the icing evenly over the top of the cake. Sprinkle with chopped walnuts, if you like, then leave until set. Serve in slices.

Sugar & Spice Cake

Makes 12–14 slices

175g unsalted butter, softened
250g soft light brown sugar
2 eggs, beaten
250g plain flour
½ teaspoon baking powder
1 teaspoon ground cinnamon
½ teaspoon freshly grated nutmeg
½ teaspoon ground ginger
Pinch of salt
1–2 tablespoons milk
1 tablespoon demerara sugar

Tip
This cake can be cut into slices and frozen so that a few slices can be defrosted and used as a quick dessert with fresh fruit and ice cream.

1 Preheat the oven to 180°C/350°F/Gas mark 4. Grease and base line a 900g loaf tin.

2 Beat the butter in a bowl until pale and creamy, then add the soft brown sugar and beat for a further 3–4 minutes. Gradually add the eggs, beating well after each addition. Sift the flour, baking powder, cinnamon, nutmeg, ginger and salt over the creamed mixture and fold in, gradually adding the milk at the same time.

3 Pour the mixture evenly into the prepared tin, then sprinkle the demerara sugar over the top. Bake in the oven for 50–55 minutes, or until firm to the touch and a skewer inserted into the centre comes out clean. Cool in the tin for 5 minutes, then turn out onto a wire rack and leave to cool completely. Serve in slices.

Chocolate Marble Cake

Makes 6–8 slices

175g self-raising flour
2 teaspoons baking powder
Pinch of salt
75g unsalted butter, softened
200g caster sugar
2 eggs, beaten
125ml milk
1 teaspoon vanilla extract
75g dark bitter chocolate, melted
175g icing sugar
4 tablespoons unsweetened cocoa
  powder

Tip
To decorate, melt a little white chocolate, spoon over the icing before it has set and swirl into the icing with a cocktail stick.

1 Preheat the oven to 180°C/350°F/Gas mark 4. Grease and base line a 20cm angel cake tin.

2 Sift the flour, baking powder and salt into a bowl and set aside. Cream the butter and caster sugar together in a separate bowl until pale and fluffy, then gradually, beating well after each addition, add the beaten eggs, a little at a time. Fold the flour mixture and milk alternately into the creamed mixture, then stir in the vanilla extract.

3 Pour half of the mixture into a separate bowl and stir in the melted chocolate. Spoon the two different batters alternately into the prepared tin, then draw a knife through the mixture to create a swirled marble effect.

4 Bake in the oven for 35–40 minutes, or until the cake is firm to the touch and a skewer inserted into the centre comes out clean. Cool the cake in the tin for 5 minutes, then turn out onto a wire rack and leave to cool completely.

5 Sift the icing sugar and cocoa powder into a bowl, then stir in enough warm water, mixing to form a thick pouring consistency. Spread or drizzle the icing evenly over the top of the cake. Serve in slices.

Rocky Road Cake

Makes 8–10 slices

225g self-raising flour
2 teaspoons baking powder
4 tablespoons unsweetened cocoa
  powder
Pinch of salt
225g unsalted butter, softened
250g caster sugar
4 eggs, beaten
6 tablespoons buttermilk
2 teaspoons vanilla extract

For the filling & topping
35 chocolate-covered caramels
3 tablespoons milk
125g mini marshmallows
100g walnuts, chopped

1 Preheat the oven to 180°C/350°F/Gas mark 4. Grease and base line two 20cm round sandwich cake tins.

2 For the cake, sift the flour, baking powder, cocoa powder and salt into a bowl. In a separate bowl, beat the butter until pale and fluffy. Add the sugar and beat for a further 2 minutes. Gradually add the eggs, beating well after each addition, then stir in the buttermilk and vanilla extract.

3 Stir in the dry ingredients, mixing well. Spoon the mixture into the prepared tins, dividing it evenly, and level the surface. Bake in the oven for 30–35 minutes, or until firm to the touch. Turn the cakes out onto a wire rack and leave to cool.

4 Cut small slits into the top of each sponge cake and set aside. For the filling and topping, put the chocolate caramels in a saucepan with the milk and 25g of the marshmallows and heat gently until melted, stirring. Put one sponge cake on a plate or cake stand and pour over half of the melted chocolate mixture. Sprinkle over half of the walnuts.

5 Place the second sponge cake on top and pour over the remaining chocolate mixture. Sprinkle with the remaining marshmallows and walnuts. Serve in slices.

Tip
Top the cake with any decorations of your choice, such as chocolate-covered caramels, milk chocolate buttons, marshmallows and/or nuts.

Jelly Bean Swiss Roll

Makes 6–8 slices

100g self-raising flour
1½ teaspoons baking powder
Pinch of salt
3 eggs
150g caster sugar, plus 2 tablespoons
½ teaspoon vanilla extract
2 tablespoons semi-skimmed milk
6 tablespoons strawberry jam
50g unsalted butter, softened
125g icing sugar, sifted
Jelly beans, to decorate

1 Preheat the oven to 190°C/375°F/Gas mark 5. Grease and line a 28 x 23cm Swiss roll tin.

2 Sift the flour, baking powder and salt into a bowl and set aside. Using a hand-held electric mixer, whisk the eggs and 150g of the caster sugar together in a large bowl until the mixture is pale, creamy and thick enough to leave a trail on the surface when the whisk is lifted. Stir in the vanilla extract and milk.

3 Gently fold the dry ingredients into the egg mixture, then pour the mixture evenly into the prepared tin. Bake in the oven for 8–10 minutes, or until just firm to the touch.

4 Sprinkle a sheet of greaseproof paper with the remaining 2 tablespoons of caster sugar and turn the sponge out onto it. Peel away the lining paper, then roll up the sponge from a long side, with the greaseproof paper inside. Transfer to a wire rack and leave to cool for 10–15 minutes.

5 Unroll the sponge cake and discard the greaseproof paper, then spread the sponge evenly with the strawberry jam and re-roll tightly. Beat the butter in a bowl until pale and fluffy, then beat in the icing sugar, mixing well. Using a piping bag fitted with a plain nozzle, pipe the butter icing over the Swiss roll and decorate with jelly beans. Serve in slices.

Tip

Instead of jam, try lemon or orange curd, chocolate spread or even marshmallow cream.

Cherry Loaf Cake

Makes 12–14 slices

225g plain flour
1 teaspoon baking powder
250g unsalted butter, softened
200g caster sugar
3 eggs, beaten
3 tablespoons semi-skimmed milk
1 teaspoon vanilla extract
50g ground almonds
150g glacé cherries, halved

Tip
To stop glacé cherries sinking, wash and pat them dry before using.

1 Preheat the oven to 180°C/350°F/Gas mark 4. Grease and base line a 900g loaf tin.

2 Sift the flour and baking powder into a bowl. In a separate bowl, cream the butter and sugar together until pale and fluffy. Gradually beat in the eggs, milk and vanilla extract, beating well after each addition. Fold in the flour mixture, ground almonds and glacé cherries.

3 Spoon the mixture into the prepared tin and level the surface. Bake in the oven for 50-55 minutes, or until firm to the touch and a skewer inserted into the centre comes out clean. Cool in the tin for 10 minutes, then turn out onto a wire rack and leave to cool completely. Serve in slices.

Apricot Frangipane Cake

Makes 8–10 slices

125g unsalted butter or margarine,
softened
125g caster sugar
½ teaspoon almond essence
100g plain flour
1 teaspoon baking powder
60g ground almonds
2 eggs
8 fresh ripe apricots, halved and
stoned
2 tablespoons apricot jam
30g flaked almonds, to decorate

1 Preheat the oven to 180°C/350°F/Gas mark 4. Grease and base line a 23cm springform tin fitted with a flat base.

2 Cream the butter or margarine and sugar together in a bowl until pale and fluffy. Beat in the almond extract. Set aside. Combine the flour, baking powder and ground almonds in a separate bowl. In another bowl, using a hand-held electric mixer, whisk the eggs until they are pale, creamy and thick.

3 Fold the dry ingredients into the creamed mixture alternately with the whisked eggs. Spoon the mixture into the prepared tin and level the surface, then arrange the apricot halves, cut-side up, over the top.

4 Bake in the oven for 35 minutes, or until risen and golden. Cool in the tin for 10 minutes, then carefully remove the cake from the tin and place it on a wire rack, apricot-side uppermost. Cool for a further 10 minutes.

5 Meanwhile, melt the apricot jam with 2 teaspoons of water in a small saucepan over a low heat. Press the mixture through a sieve into a bowl. Brush the top of the warm cake with the apricot glaze, then scatter the flaked almonds on top. Serve warm or cold in slices.

Lemon & Ginger Cake

Makes 12–14 slices

250g plain flour
1 teaspoon baking powder
250g unsalted butter, softened
200g caster sugar
3 eggs, beaten
3 tablespoons semi-skimmed milk
50g ground almonds
1 teaspoon ground ginger
2 tablespoons finely grated lemon zest
2 tablespoons finely grated candied
    lemon peel

1 Preheat the oven to 180°C/350°F/Gas mark 4. Grease and base line a 900g loaf tin.

2 Sift the flour and baking powder into a bowl. In a separate bowl, cream the butter and sugar together until pale and fluffy. Gradually beat in the eggs and milk, then fold in the flour mixture, ground almonds, ginger and lemon zest.

3 Spoon the mixture into the prepared tin and level the surface. Bake in the oven for 55–60 minutes, or until firm to the touch and a skewer inserted into the centre comes out clean.

4 Cool in the tin for 10 minutes, then turn out onto a wire rack and leave to cool completely. Spoon the candied lemon peel evenly over the top of the cake. Serve in slices.

Tip

To make your own candied peel, place pared strips of unwaxed lemon peel from 2 lemons in a small saucepan of water and bring to the boil. Drain and refresh under cold water. Repeat this process. Finely shred the peel and return it to the pan with enough water to cover and 100g of caster sugar. Heat gently to dissolve the sugar, then bring to the boil and simmer until the syrup thickens. Remove the pan from the heat and cool slightly.

Caribbean Banana Bread

Makes 6–8 slices

2 bananas, peeled
2 tablespoons clear honey
200g self-raising flour
½ teaspoon baking powder
1 teaspoon freshly grated nutmeg
150g unsalted butter, softened
175g soft light brown sugar
2 eggs, beaten
50g pecan nuts, finely chopped

1 Preheat the oven to 180°C/350°F/Gas mark 4. Grease and base line a 450g loaf tin.

2 Mash the bananas in a bowl with the honey. Sift the flour, baking powder and nutmeg into a separate bowl.

3 Cream the butter and sugar together in a large bowl until pale and fluffy, then gradually add the eggs, beating well after each addition.

4 Fold in the bananas and the flour mixture together with the pecan nuts. Spoon the mixture into the prepared tin and level the surface. Bake in the oven for 50-60 minutes, or until risen and golden and a skewer inserted into the centre comes out clean.

5 Cool in the tin for 10 minutes, then turn out onto a wire rack and leave to cool completely. Serve in slices.

Apple, Cranberry & Cider Cake

Makes 6–8 slices

3 medium red-skinned eating apples
100g dried sweetened cranberries
200ml dry cider
350g self-raising flour
2 teaspoons ground cinnamon
175g light muscovado sugar
175g unsalted butter, melted
3 eggs, beaten

For the topping
1 medium red-skinned eating apple,
   thinly sliced and pips removed
3 tablespoons apricot jam, warmed

Tip
Use apple juice
in place of the cider
for a non-alcoholic
alternative.

1 For the cake, peel and core the apples, then chop them roughly. Put the apples, cranberries and cider in a saucepan and bring to the boil, then simmer very gently for 5 minutes. Remove the pan from the heat and set aside to cool completely.

2 Preheat the oven to 180°C/350°F/Gas mark 4. Grease and base line a 20cm springform tin fitted with a flat base.

3 Sift the flour and cinnamon into a bowl and stir in the sugar. Add the melted butter, eggs and apple and cider mixture. Stir until just combined, then spoon into the prepared tin and level the surface. For the topping, arrange the apple slices evenly over the top of the cake mixture.

4 Bake in the oven for 50–60 minutes, or until a skewer inserted into the centre comes out clean. Leave to cool in the tin for 5 minutes, then turn out onto a wire rack.

5 Brush the apricot jam over the top of the cake while it is still warm. Leave to cool completely, then serve in slices.

Orange & Almond
Sponge Cake

Makes 6–8 slices

175g unsalted butter, softened
175g caster sugar
3 eggs, beaten
150g self-raising flour
50g ground almonds
Few drops of almond extract

For the icing & decoration
280g cream cheese or full-fat
   soft cheese
2 tablespoons freshly squeezed orange
   juice
2 teaspoons finely grated orange zest
100g icing sugar, sifted
Toasted flaked almonds and thinly
   pared orange zest, to decorate

1 Preheat the oven to 190°C/375°F/Gas mark 5. Grease and base line two 20cm round sandwich cake tins.

2 For the cake, beat the butter and sugar together in a bowl until pale and fluffy. Gradually add the eggs, beating well after each addition. Sift the flour over the creamed mixture, then gently fold in with the ground almonds and almond extract until well combined.

3 Spoon the mixture into the prepared tins, dividing it evenly, then level the surface. Bake in the oven for 20–25 minutes, or until risen and golden and the centres of the cakes spring back when lightly pressed. Turn out onto a wire rack and leave to cool.

4 Meanwhile, to make the icing, beat the cream cheese or soft cheese in a bowl to soften. Add the orange juice, orange zest and icing sugar and beat together until smooth and creamy.

5 Sandwich the two cakes together with a little icing, then spread the remaining icing over the top of the cake. Scatter with toasted, flaked almonds and orange zest to decorate. Serve in slices.

Gooey Chocolate Cake

Makes 8–10 slices

300g dark bitter chocolate (at least 70% cocoa solids), broken into squares
175g unsalted butter, cut into small pieces
8 eggs, separated
200g soft light brown sugar
60g ground almonds

For the topping & decoration
125g plain chocolate, melted
125g milk chocolate, melted
Chocolate-dipped fresh strawberries, to decorate

1 Preheat the oven to 180°C/350°F/Gas mark 4. Grease a 20cm springform tin fitted with a flat base, then line the base and side of the tin with foil.

2 For the cake, melt the chocolate and butter in a large, heat-proof bowl set over a pan of barely simmering water. Remove from heat and leave to cool.

3 In a separate bowl, using a hand-held electric mixer, whisk the egg yolks and sugar together until thick and pale. Stir in the cooled chocolate and butter mixture, then stir in the ground almonds.

4 In another bowl, whisk the egg whites until stiff, then fold them into the chocolate mixture. Pour the mixture evenly into the prepared tin. Place the tin in a roasting tin half full of boiling water.

5 Place in the oven and bake for 1–1¼ hours, or until the cake is quite firm, yet a skewer inserted into the centre comes out a little sticky. Remove the cake from the oven and leave to cool completely in the tin, then turn out and place on a serving plate.

6 For the topping, drizzle the melted plain and milk chocolates decoratively over the cake. Decorate with chocolate-dipped strawberries and leave to set. Serve in slices.

Angel Food Cake

Makes 8–10 slices

50g plain flour
1 tablespoon cornflour
200g caster sugar
7 egg whites
¾ teaspoon cream of tartar
Pinch of salt
1½ teaspoons vanilla extract

For the icing & decoration
2 egg whites
350g caster sugar
¼ teaspoon cream of tartar
2 tablespoons toasted chopped
    pistachio nuts, to decorate

1 Preheat the oven to 180°C/350°F/Gas mark 4. Grease and line a 23cm springform tin fitted with a tube base.

2 For the cake, sift the flour and cornflour into a bowl. Add 65g of the sugar and sift the ingredients together twice.

3 In a separate large bowl, whisk the egg whites until foamy. Add the cream of tartar and salt and whisk until stiff. Whisk the remaining sugar into the egg whites until the mixture is stiff and glossy. Whisk in the vanilla extract.

4 Carefully fold in the flour mixture, then spoon the batter into the prepared tin and level the surface. Bake in the oven for 45-50 minutes, or until pale golden and the top springs back when lightly pressed. Place the cake tin on a wire rack and leave to cool in the tin.

5 Meanwhile, to make the icing, put all the icing ingredients in a heat-proof bowl, add 4 tablespoons of water and set the bowl over a pan of barely simmering water. Using a hand-held electric mixer, whisk the mixture for 10-12 minutes, or until thick.

6 Run a knife around the inside edge of the tin and remove the cold cake. Spread the icing evenly over the top and sides of the cake and sprinkle with the pistachio nuts. Leave to set, then serve in slices.

Plum & Amaretti
Sponge Cake

Makes 24 squares

175g unsalted butter, softened
175g caster sugar
3 large eggs
175g self-raising flour, sifted
2 teaspoons finely grated lemon zest
1 tablespoon freshly squeezed lemon juice
6 plums, halved and stoned
25g amaretti biscuits, coarsely crushed
1 tablespoon demerara sugar, for sprinkling

Tip
When in season try blackberry and apple to ring the changes.

1 Preheat the oven to 180°C/350°F/Gas mark 4. Grease and line a 28 x 18cm square cake tin.

2 Cream the butter and caster sugar together in a bowl until pale and fluffy. Gradually add the eggs, beating well after each addition. Sift the flour over the creamed mixture and fold in together with the lemon zest and juice, mixing well.

3 Spoon the mixture into the prepared tin and level the surface. Arrange the plum halves, cut-side down, over the top, then sprinkle with the crushed amaretti and demerara sugar.

4 Bake in the oven for 45–50 minutes, or until risen and golden. Cool slightly in the tin, then turn out onto a wire rack, invert the cake so that the plums are on top and leave to cool. Serve warm or cold cut into squares.

Coconut Cream Cake

Makes 8–10 slices

125g unsalted butter, softened
150g caster sugar
250ml buttermilk
1 teaspoon vanilla extract
200g plain flour
1 teaspoon baking powder
½ teaspoon bicarbonate of soda
Pinch of salt
100g flaked or desiccated coconut
4 egg whites

1 Preheat the oven to 180°C/350°F/Gas mark 4. Grease and base line a deep 23cm round cake tin.

2 Cream the butter and sugar together in a bowl until pale and fluffy, then mix in the buttermilk and vanilla extract. Sift the flour, baking powder, bicarbonate of soda and salt into the bowl and fold in until combined. Add the coconut, reserving 2 tablespoons, and mix well.

3 In a separate bowl, whisk the egg whites until stiff. Stir one-third of the whisked egg whites into the cake mixture to loosen it, then fold in the remainder. Pour the mixture evenly into the prepared tin and sprinkle with the reserved 2 tablespoons of coconut.

4 Bake in the oven for 30–35 minutes, or until golden and firm to the touch. Turn out onto a wire rack and leave to cool. Serve in slices.

Tip
To revive dry coconut flakes, cover with milk and refrigerate for a couple of hours. Drain and pat dry before using.

Date & Walnut Loaf

Makes 12–14 slices

125g unsalted butter, cut into small
pieces
125g light muscovado sugar
50g golden syrup
150ml milk
2 large eggs, beaten
250g plain flour
1 level teaspoon bicarbonate of soda
1 teaspoon ground mixed spice
150g stoned dried dates, chopped
50g walnuts, chopped

For the topping
50g stoned dried dates, chopped
25g walnuts, chopped
1 tablespoon caster sugar
1 teaspoon ground cinnamon

1 Preheat the oven to 150°C/300°F/Gas mark 2. Grease and base line a 900g loaf tin.

2 For the cake, put the butter, sugar and golden syrup in a large saucepan and heat gently, stirring. When the butter has melted, remove the pan from the heat and set aside to cool for a few minutes.

3 Stir the milk and eggs into the cooled syrup mixture. Sift the flour, bicarbonate of soda and mixed spice into a bowl, then stir in the syrup mixture. Mix to a smooth batter, then fold in the dates and walnuts.

4 Pour the mixture evenly into the prepared tin. Mix the topping ingredients together and sprinkle thickly over the top of the cake.

5 Bake in the oven for 1–1¼ hours, or until a skewer inserted into the centre comes out clean. Cool in the tin for 5 minutes, then turn out onto a wire rack and leave to cool completely. Serve in slices.

Apple Crumb Cake

Makes 6–8 slices

140g unsalted butter
450g cooking apples, peeled, cored
and chopped
½ teaspoon freshly grated nutmeg
1 teaspoon ground cinnamon
225g plain flour
150g caster sugar
2 eggs, beaten
3 tablespoons soured cream
1 teaspoon vanilla extract
½ teaspoon baking powder
¼ teaspoon bicarbonate of soda
Pinch of salt

1 Preheat the oven to 180°C/350°F/Gas mark 4. Grease and base line a deep 20cm round cake tin.

2 Melt 25g of the butter in a small saucepan. Add the apples, sprinkle in the nutmeg and half of the cinnamon and stir to coat the apples in the butter. Place a disc of non-stick baking paper on top of the apples, reduce the heat and cook gently, stirring occasionally, for 5–10 minutes, or until the apples are tender. Remove the pan from the heat.

3 In a bowl, lightly rub 25g of the flour, 25g of the remaining butter and 25g of the sugar together, until the mixture resembles coarse. Set this crumb topping aside.

4 In a separate bowl, cream the remaining butter and sugar together until pale and fluffy, then gradually beat in the eggs, beating well after each addition. Beat in the soured cream and vanilla extract.

5 Sift the remaining flour and cinnamon, the baking powder, bicarbonate of soda and salt into the creamed mixture and fold in gently.

6 Stir in the warm apples, then spoon the mixture into the prepared tin and level the surface. Sprinkle over the reserved crumb topping. Bake in the oven for 40–45 minutes, or until a skewer inserted into the centre comes out clean. Turn out onto a wire rack and leave to cool. Serve in slices.

Tip

Serve this cake as a pudding with vanilla ice cream or a creamy custard.

Pineapple Upside-Down Cake

Makes 8–10 slices

50g unsalted butter, softened
100g soft light brown sugar
425g can pineapple rings in natural
    juice, drained
7 glacé cherries
50g toasted flaked almonds (optional)
200g caster sugar
3 eggs, separated
5 tablespoons pineapple juice
½ teaspoon vanilla extract
¼ teaspoon almond extract
150g self-raising flour, sifted
1 teaspoon baking powder
⅛ teaspoon salt
Single cream, to serve

1 Preheat the oven to 180°C/350°F/ Gas mark 4. Grease and base line a deep 23cm round cake tin. Reserve 15g of the butter, then melt the remainder in a saucepan over a low heat. Pour into the prepared tin and sprinkle the brown sugar evenly over it.

2 Arrange the pineapple rings in the butter-sugar mixture, placing a glacé cherry in the centre of each ring. Sprinkle the flaked almonds over the top, if using.

3 Cream the reserved butter and the caster sugar together in a bowl until pale and fluffy, then gradually beat in the egg yolks, beating well after each addition. Add the pineapple juice, then the vanilla and almond extracts, mixing well. Sift the flour, baking powder and salt into the creamed mixture and fold in, mixing well.

4 In a separate bowl, whisk the egg whites until stiff, then fold them into the creamed mixture. Spoon the mixture evenly over the pineapple base in the tin.

5 Bake in the oven for 30–35 minutes, or until firm to the touch. Remove the cake from the oven and leave to cool in the tin. Loosen the cake and invert onto a serving plate so that the pineapple and cherry base is now on top. Serve the cake warm or cold in slices with single cream.

Gooseberry
& Elderflower Cake

Makes 8–10 slices

280g self-raising flour
1 teaspoon baking powder
100g caster sugar
125g soft light brown sugar
125g unsalted butter, melted
2 eggs, beaten
350g cooked unsweetened gooseberries
2 tablespoons elderflower cordial

For the icing
125g icing sugar, sifted
3–5 teaspoons elderflower cordial

Tip
When in season, decorate the cake with fresh elderflowers, carefully rinsed, patted dry and dusted with icing sugar.

1 Preheat the oven to 180°C/350°F/Gas mark 4. Grease and base line a 23cm springform tin fitted with a flat base.

2 For the cake, mix the flour, baking powder and sugars together in a bowl. Add the melted butter and eggs and mix well. Stir in the gooseberries and elderflower cordial until well combined. Spoon the mixture into the prepared tin and level the surface.

3 Bake in the oven for about 45 minutes, or until a skewer inserted into the centre comes out clean. Cool in the tin for 5 minutes, then turn out onto a wire rack and leave to cool completely.

4 When the cake is cold, make the icing. Put the icing sugar in a bowl and stir in just enough elderflower cordial to make a thick pouring consistency. Using a teaspoon, drizzle the icing randomly and decoratively over the top of the cake. Leave to set, then serve in slices.

Chocolate & Strawberry
Layer Cake

Makes 8–10 slices

250g dark bitter chocolate, chopped
175ml milk
250g unsalted butter, softened
225g soft dark brown sugar
3 eggs, beaten
200g self-raising flour
1 tablespoon baking powder
4 tablespoons unsweetened cocoa
    powder
4 tablespoons strawberry compote or
    strawberry jam
50g icing sugar

1 Preheat the oven to 170°C/325°F/Gas mark 3. Grease and base line two 20cm round sandwich cake tins. Melt 100g of the chocolate and the milk together in a heat-proof bowl set over a pan of barely simmering water. Remove from the heat and set aside.

2 Cream 125g of the butter and all of the brown sugar together in a bowl until pale and fluffy, then gradually beat in the eggs, beating well after each addition.

3 Sift the flour, baking powder and cocoa powder into a separate bowl. Fold the flour mixture into the creamed mixture alternately with the chocolate milk.

4 Divide the mixture evenly between the prepared tins and level the surface. Bake in the oven for 25–30 minutes, or until firm to the touch. Turn out onto a wire rack and leave to cool.

5 Melt and cool the remaining chocolate. Sandwich the two cakes together with the strawberry compote or strawberry jam. Cream the remaining butter in a bowl, then beat in the icing sugar. Pour in the melted, cooled chocolate and mix well. Spread the chocolate icing over the top of the cake. Serve in slices.

Coffee, Maple & Pecan
Sponge Cake

Makes 6-8 slices

75g plain flour
Pinch of salt
40g unsalted butter, melted
3 large eggs
75g caster sugar
1 teaspoon instant coffee granules
½ teaspoon vanilla extract

For the icing & decoration
175g unsalted butter, softened
100g icing sugar
1 teaspoon instant coffee granules
4 tablespoons maple syrup
8 pecan nut halves, to decorate

1 Preheat the oven to 180ºC/350ºF/Gas mark 4. Grease and line a deep 20cm round cake tin. Sift the flour and salt together three times into a bowl and set aside.

2 Using a hand-held electric mixer, whisk the eggs and sugar together in a large, heat-proof bowl set over a pan of barely simmering water until the mixture is pale, creamy and thick enough to leave a trail on the surface when the whisk is lifted.

3 In a small bowl, dissolve the coffee in 1 tablespoon of hot water, then whisk this into the egg mixture together with the vanilla extract. Sift the seasoned flour over the egg mixture in three batches, drizzling a little of the melted butter around the edge of the mixture in between each batch, and carefully fold in.

4 Pour the mixture evenly into the prepared tin. Bake in the oven for 25-30 minutes, or until risen and golden. Cool in the tin for 2-3 minutes, then turn the cake out onto a wire rack and leave to cool completely.

5 Meanwhile, for the icing, beat the butter and icing sugar together in a bowl until smooth. In a small bowl, dissolve the coffee in 1 tablespoon of hot water, then gradually beat this into the creamed mixture together with the maple syrup until smooth and well mixed.

6 Cut the cake in half horizontally twice to make three layers. Sandwich the cake layers together with some of the icing, then spread the remaining icing over the top and sides of the cake. Decorate the top with pecan nut halves. Serve in slices.

Caramel Pecan Loaf

Makes 8–10 slices

450g strong plain white flour
15g cold unsalted butter, cut into small
   pieces
2 teaspoons salt
1½ teaspoons easy-blend dried yeast
300ml warmed water

For the filling & topping
175g unsalted butter, softened
175g soft light brown sugar
100g pecan nuts, roughly chopped
2 tablespoons double cream

1 Generously grease a 23cm springform tin fitted with a flat base. Sift the flour into a large bowl, then rub in the butter. Stir in the salt and yeast, then make a well in the centre and add the water. Mix to a soft dough, then knead for about 10 minutes, or until smooth. Shape into a ball and put into a clean oiled bowl. Cover and leave to rise in a warm place for about 1 hour, or until doubled in size.

2 Knead the dough again briefly for about 1 minute on a lightly floured surface, then pat out to form a 25 x 35cm rectangle. Trim to a neat shape. Cover and leave to rest for 10 minutes. Preheat the oven to 200°C/400°F/Gas mark 6.

3 Meanwhile, for the filling and topping, cream 100g of the butter and 100g of the sugar together in a bowl until smooth. Stir in most of the pecan nuts. Spread the mixture evenly over the dough, leaving a 2.5cm margin around the edges. Starting from a long side, roll up the dough tightly and cut into 5cm slices. Arrange the slices in the prepared tin, cut-side up. Cover and leave to rise in a warm place for about 30 minutes, or until the dough has risen to the top of the tin.

4 Bake the loaf in the oven for 30–40 minutes, or until risen and golden, covering the top with foil if it begins to over-brown.

5 Meanwhile, melt the remaining butter and sugar together in a saucepan over a low heat. Add the cream and bring to the boil. Simmer for 3–4 minutes, then add the remaining pecan nuts and cook for 1 minute. Remove from the heat.

6 Remove the loaf from the oven and immediately spread the pecan mixture evenly over the top. Cool in the tin, then turn out and serve in slices.

Hazelnut Meringue Cake

Makes 8–10 slices

4 egg whites
200g caster sugar
1 teaspoon vanilla extract
1 teaspoon cider vinegar
1 teaspoon cornflour
80g toasted hazelnuts, finely ground
2 tablespoons coarsely chopped
   toasted hazelnuts

For the filling
75g natural yoghurt
2 tablespoons bourbon
2 tablespoons clear honey
125ml double or whipping cream
225g fresh raspberries
Sifted icing sugar, for dusting

1 Preheat the oven to 180°C/350°F/Gas mark 4. Grease and base line two 20cm round sandwich cake tins.

2 For the meringue, whisk the egg whites in a bowl until stiff peaks form. Gradually whisk in the sugar to make a stiff and glossy meringue. Fold in the vanilla extract, vinegar, cornflour and ground hazelnuts.

3 Divide the mixture evenly between the two prepared tins and level the surface. Scatter the chopped hazelnuts over the top of one, then bake in the oven for 50–60 minutes, or until crisp. Turn out onto a wire rack and leave to cool.

4 For the filling, stir the yoghurt, bourbon and honey together in a bowl. In a separate bowl, whip the cream until soft peaks form, then fold into the yoghurt mixture with the raspberries.

5 Sandwich the two meringues together with the cream mixture, with the nut-topped meringue uppermost. Dust with sifted icing sugar. Serve in slices.

Chocolate Refrigerator
Cake

Makes 12–14 slices

450g dark bitter chocolate, broken into
squares

250g unsalted butter, cut into small
pieces

350g shortbread biscuits or digestive
biscuits, roughly chopped

200g pecan nuts, chopped

150g raisins

150g glacé cherries, halved

50g mini marshmallows

1 Grease and line a 900g loaf tin with a double
layer of cling film.

2 Melt the chocolate and butter together in a
large, heat-proof bowl set over a pan of barely
simmering water. Remove the bowl from the heat.
Add all the remaining ingredients and stir together
until well mixed.

3 Spoon the mixture into the prepared tin
and level the surface. Cover and refrigerate
for 2-3 hours, or until firm enough to turn out.
Serve in slices.

Tip
You can vary the
ingredients according to what
you have to hand, such as using
plain or milk chocolate, other
varieties of biscuit, walnuts or
mixed nuts and sultanas or
dried mixed fruit.

Iced Lime Traybake

Makes 16–18 squares

225g unsalted butter, softened
225g caster sugar
225g self-raising flour
1 teaspoon baking powder
4 large eggs
2 teaspoons finely grated lime zest
10–12 sugar cubes, crushed

For the topping
Thinly pared zest of 2 limes and the
   juice of 3 limes
100g granulated sugar

1 Preheat the oven to 180°C/350°F/Gas mark 4. Lightly grease and line a 28 x 18cm cake tin or baking tin.

2 For the cake, put all the ingredients except the crushed sugar cubes into a large bowl and beat together until smooth, light and well mixed. Turn the mixture into the prepared tin and level the surface. Sprinkle the crushed sugar cubes evenly over the top.

3 Bake in the oven for 40 minutes, or until well risen, golden and the top springs back when lightly pressed.

4 Mix the topping ingredients together in a bowl. Remove the cake from the oven and pour the sugar topping evenly over the cake. Leave the cake to cool completely in the tin, then turn out and cut into squares to serve.

New York Cheesecake

Makes 12–14 slices

200g digestive biscuits, crushed
50g unsalted butter, melted
900g cream cheese or full-fat soft
   cheese
Pinch of salt
300g caster sugar
250ml soured cream
2 teaspoons vanilla extract
1 tablespoon finely grated lemon zest
1 tablespoon freshly squeezed lemon
   juice
4 eggs, beaten
2 egg yolks

1 Preheat the oven to 150°C/300°F/Gas mark 2. Grease a 23cm springform tin fitted with a flat base.

2 In a bowl, mix the biscuit crumbs and melted butter together, then press this mixture evenly into the base of the prepared tin. Bake in the oven for 10 minutes, or until lightly browned, then remove from the oven and set aside to cool.

3 In a separate bowl, beat the cream cheese or soft cheese until soft and smooth. Add the salt and sugar and beat for 1 minute. Add the soured cream, vanilla extract, lemon zest and lemon juice and beat for a further 1 minute. Add the eggs and egg yolks and beat until well combined. Pour the mixture evenly over the biscuit base in the tin.

4 Bake in the oven for 45–50 minutes, or until set at the edges but slightly soft in the centre. Turn off the oven, but leave the cheesecake inside with the door ajar for 45 minutes.

5 Remove the cheesecake from the oven and cool to room temperature. Remove from the tin, place on a serving plate, cover with foil and refrigerate for at least 4 hours, or preferably overnight, before serving in slices.

Dark Chocolate
Cheesecake

Makes 12–14 slices

200g digestive biscuits, crushed
50g unsalted butter, melted
675g cream cheese or full-fat soft
   cheese
Pinch of salt
3 tablespoons cornflour
200g caster sugar
2 eggs, beaten
2 egg yolks
2 teaspoons vanilla extract
350ml whipping cream
125ml soured cream
275g dark bitter chocolate, melted
6 tablespoons unsweetened cocoa
   powder, sifted, plus extra for dusting
2 tablespoons chocolate shards
   or curls

1 Preheat the oven to 150°C/300°F/Gas mark 2. Grease a 23cm springform tin fitted with a flat base.

2 In a small bowl, mix the biscuit crumbs and melted butter together, then press this mixture evenly into the base of the prepared tin. Bake in the oven for 10 minutes, or until lightly browned, then remove from the oven and set aside to cool.

3 Beat the cream cheese or soft cheese in a large bowl until soft and smooth. Add the salt, cornflour and sugar and beat together for 1 minute. Gradually add the eggs and egg yolks, beating well to combine. Stir in the vanilla extract. Lightly whip the cream in a separate bowl. Fold the whipped cream and soured cream into the cheese mixture.

4 Stir in the melted chocolate and sifted cocoa powder, mixing well. Pour the mixture evenly over the biscuit base in the tin. Bake in the oven for 55-60 minutes, or until set at the edges but slightly soft in the centre. Turn off the oven, but leave the cheesecake inside with the door ajar for 45 minutes.

5 Remove the cheesecake from the oven and cool to room temperature. Remove from the tin, place on a serving plate, cover with foil and refrigerate until cold. Decorate the cheesecake with chocolate shards or curls and dust with extra sifted cocoa powder before serving in slices.

Lady Baltimore Cake

Makes 12 slices

250g unsalted butter, softened
250g caster sugar
1 teaspoon vanilla extract
300g plain flour
1 tablespoon baking powder
¼ teaspoon salt
250ml milk
6 egg whites

For the icing
400g caster sugar
2 tablespoons golden syrup
4 egg whites
Pinch of cream of tartar
75g raisins
50g pecan nuts, chopped
75g glacé cherries, chopped
1 teaspoon vanilla extract

1 Preheat the oven to 180°C/350°F/Gas mark 4. Grease and flour two 23cm round sandwich cake tins. Cream the butter, 200g of the sugar and the vanilla extract together in a bowl until pale and fluffy. Sift the flour, baking powder and salt into a separate bowl. Fold the flour mixture and milk alternately into the creamed mixture.

2 In a separate bowl, whisk the egg whites until soft peaks form, then add the remaining 50g sugar and whisk until the mixture is stiff and glossy. Stir one-third of the whisked egg whites into the cake mixture to loosen it, then gently fold in the remainder. Pour the mixture into the prepared tins, dividing it evenly.

3 Bake in the oven for 25–30 minutes, or until the cakes are golden and just firm to the touch. Turn out onto a wire rack and leave to cool.

4 To make the icing, put the sugar in a medium, heavy-based saucepan with the golden syrup and 6 tablespoons of water. Stir to dissolve the sugar over a medium heat. Cook the sugar to medium ball stage, 118°C/245°F, without stirring. Meanwhile, whisk the egg whites and cream of tartar together in a heat-proof bowl. When the sugar syrup has reached the correct temperature, pour it steadily into the egg whites, whisking continuously. Continue to whisk for 5 minutes, or until the icing is thick and creamy.

5 Stir the raisins, glacé cherries, pecan nuts and vanilla extract into the cooled icing and use to sandwich the cakes together. Spread over the top and sides, leave to set, then serve in slices.

Whipped Cream
Cheesecake

Makes 12–14 slices

200g digestive biscuits, crushed
50g unsalted butter, melted
675g cream cheese or full-fat
 soft cheese
Pinch of salt
3 tablespoons cornflour
200g caster sugar
2 eggs, beaten
2 egg yolks
2 teaspoons vanilla extract
1 teaspoon seeds from a vanilla pod
 (optional)
600ml whipping cream
Fresh fruit, to decorate

1 Preheat the oven to 150°C/300°F/Gas mark 2.
Grease a 23cm springform tin fitted with a flat base. Mix the biscuit crumbs and melted butter together and press evenly into the base of the prepared tin. Bake in the oven for 10 minutes, or until lightly browned, then remove from the oven and set aside to cool.

2 Beat the cream cheese or soft cheese in a large bowl until soft and smooth. Add the salt, cornflour and sugar and beat together for 1 minute. Gradually add the eggs and egg yolks, beating well to combine. Stir in the vanilla extract and vanilla seeds, if using.

3 In a separate bowl, whip the cream until soft peaks form, then fold half of the whipped cream into the cheese mixture. Cover and refrigerate the remaining cream. Pour the soft cheese mixture evenly over the biscuit base in the tin. Bake in the oven for 50–60 minutes, or until set at the edges but slightly soft in the centre.

4 Turn off the oven, but leave the cheesecake inside with the door ajar. Cool in the oven for 30 minutes. Remove the cheesecake from the oven and cool to room temperature. Remove from the tin, place on a serving plate, cover with foil and refrigerate until cold.

5 When ready to serve spread the reserved whipped cream evenly over the top of the cheesecake and decorate with your favourite fruit. Serve in slices.

Strawberry Cake

with Flaked Almonds

Makes 10–12 slices

250g unsalted butter, softened
250g caster sugar
2 eggs, beaten
1 teaspoon vanilla extract
Pinch of salt
4 tablespoons soured cream
1 teaspoon bicarbonate of soda
225g plain flour
100g ground almonds

For the icing
350ml whipping cream
2 tablespoons icing sugar
1 teaspoon finely grated lemon zest
4 tablespoons soured cream
4 tablespoons toasted flaked almonds
450g fresh strawberries, halved and
   sliced

1 Preheat the oven to 180°C/350°F/Gas mark 4. Grease and base line a deep 23cm round cake tin.

2 For the cake, cream the butter and sugar together in a bowl until pale and fluffy. Gradually add the eggs, beating well after each addition. Stir in the vanilla extract, salt and soured cream until well combined.

3 Sift the bicarbonate of soda with the flour, then fold this into the egg mixture together with the ground almonds.

4 Spoon the mixture into the prepared tin and level the surface. Bake in the oven for 30-35 minutes, or until golden and firm to the touch. Turn out onto a wire rack and leave to cool.

5 For the icing, whip the cream in a bowl until it forms soft peaks. Add the icing sugar, lemon zest and soured cream, mixing well. Spread the icing over the top and side of the cake. Press the flaked almonds around the sides and arrange the strawberry slices on top of the cake. Refrigerate until ready to serve. Serve in slices.

Fruit Gingerbread

Makes 6–8 slices

400g plain flour

1 teaspoon baking powder

1 tablespoon ground ginger

1 teaspoon ground cinnamon

225g unsalted butter cut into small
  pieces

125g molasses or black treacle

175g soft light brown sugar

3 eggs, beaten

75g dried cherries, halved

115g stoned dried dates, chopped

50g preserved stem ginger, drained
  and chopped

90g sultanas

1 Preheat the oven to 150°C/300°F/Gas mark 2. Grease and base line a deep 20cm square cake tin.

2 Mix the flour, baking powder, ground ginger and cinnamon together in a large bowl. Set aside. Put the butter into a saucepan with the molasses or black treacle and sugar and stir over a low heat until melted. Pour into the flour mixture and mix well. Beat in the eggs until smooth, then stir in the dried cherries, dates, stem ginger and sultanas, mixing well.

3 Pour the mixture evenly into the prepared tin. Bake in the oven for 1–1¼ hours, or until a skewer inserted into the centre comes out clean. Cool in the tin for 10 minutes, then turn out onto a wire rack and leave to cool completely. Serve in slices or squares.

Golden Buttercream
Cake

Makes 8–10 slices

250g sponge (premium self-raising)
  flour
2 teaspoons baking powder
Pinch of salt
225g unsalted butter, softened
250g caster sugar
4 eggs, beaten
1 teaspoon vanilla extract

For the icing
125g unsalted butter, softened
1 teaspoon vanilla extract
200g icing sugar, sifted
3–4 drops of yellow food colouring

1 Preheat the oven to 180°C/350°F/Gas mark 4. Grease and base line two 20cm round sandwich cake tins.

2 For the cake, sift the flour, baking powder and salt into a bowl. In a separate bowl, beat the butter until pale and fluffy. Add the sugar and beat for a further 2 minutes. Gradually add the eggs, beating well after each addition. Add the vanilla extract, then fold in the flour mixture.

3 Spoon the mixture into the prepared tins, dividing it evenly, and level the surface. Bake in the oven for 30–35 minutes, or until risen, golden and firm to the touch. Turn out onto a wire rack and leave to cool.

4 For the icing, beat the butter and vanilla extract together in a bowl until pale and fluffy, then stir in the icing sugar. Add the yellow food colouring and beat to mix well. Sandwich the two cakes together with some of the icing, then spread the remaining icing over the top of the cake. Serve in slices.

Rum Cake

Makes 12–14 slices

200g unsalted butter, softened
250g soft light brown sugar
2 eggs, beaten
250g plain flour
½ teaspoon baking powder
1 teaspoon ground allspice
Pinch of salt
3 tablespoons dark rum

For the topping
50g caster sugar
3 tablespoons rum
40g unsalted butter, cut into small
   pieces

Tip
This cake will freeze well.
Simply cut into slices and
wrap individually - that way you
can take them out as and
when needed. Perfect
for lunchboxes
and picnics.

1 Preheat the oven to 180°C/350°F/Gas mark 4. Grease and base line a 900g loaf tin.

2 For the cake, beat the butter in a bowl until pale and creamy, then add the sugar and beat for a further 3-4 minutes.

3 Gradually add the eggs, beating well after each addition. Sift the flour, baking powder, allspice and salt over the creamed mixture and fold in together with the rum.

4 Spoon the mixture into the prepared tin and level the surface. Bake in the oven for 50-55 minutes, or until the cake is firm to the touch and a skewer inserted into the centre comes out clean.

5 Meanwhile, to make the topping, put the sugar, rum, butter and 2 tablespoons of water in a saucepan and heat gently, stirring until the sugar has dissolved.

6 Remove the cake from the oven. Using a cocktail stick, prick the top of the cake lightly, then pour over the rum syrup. Cool in the tin for 10-15 minutes, then turn out and serve warm or cold in slices.

Tropical Fruit Cake

Makes 8–10 slices

150g unsalted butter, softened
150g caster sugar
2 eggs, beaten
150g self-raising flour
2 tablespoons coconut cream
250g mixed ready-to-eat dried tropical
   fruit, chopped
50g macadamia nuts, chopped

1 Preheat the oven to 180°C/350°F/Gas mark 4. Grease and base line a 450g loaf tin.

2 Beat the butter and sugar together in a bowl until pale and fluffy. Gradually add the eggs, beating well after each addition. Fold in the flour, then stir in the coconut cream.

3 Stir in the dried tropical fruit and macadamia nuts. Spoon the mixture into the prepared tin and level the surface.

4 Bake in the oven for about 50 minutes, or until a skewer inserted into the centre comes out clean. Cool in the tin for 5–10 minutes, then turn out onto a wire rack and leave to cool completely. Serve in slices.

Tip

You can use chopped Brazil nuts instead of the macadamia nuts. Sprinkle the top of the cake with toasted flaked coconut to decorate as an extra topping.

Strawberry Shortcake

Makes 8 slices

400g self-raising flour
1½ tablespoons baking powder
¼ teaspoon salt
75g cold unsalted butter, cut into small
  pieces
100g caster sugar
250ml buttermilk, plus extra for
  brushing
Jam (coarse) sugar, for sprinkling

For the filling
185ml whipping cream
2 tablespoons icing sugar
½ teaspoon vanilla extract
450g fresh strawberries, halved

1 Preheat the oven to 190°C/375°F/Gas mark 5. Grease and flour a baking sheet. Sift the flour, baking powder and salt into a large bowl. Rub in the butter until the mixture resembles fine breadcrumbs.

2 Combine 65g of the caster sugar and the buttermilk in a bowl, then add this to the flour mixture. Mix to form a smooth dough, but do not overwork at this stage. Turn the dough onto a lightly floured surface and divide into two balls, one slightly larger than the other. Roll out each ball of dough to form a round about 2cm thick.

3 Place the dough rounds on the prepared baking sheet. Brush off any excess flour. Brush the tops with buttermilk and sprinkle with jam (coarse) sugar. Bake in the oven for 20–25 minutes, or until golden. Transfer the shortcake rounds to a wire rack and leave to cool completely.

4 For the filling, whip the cream in a bowl until soft peaks form, then whisk in the icing sugar and vanilla extract, mixing well. Set aside.

5 Put the strawberries in a saucepan with 2 tablespoons of water and the remaining 35g of caster sugar and heat gently for 2–3 minutes to soften the fruit. Remove the pan from the heat.

6 Spoon the whipped cream onto the larger of the cooled shortcake rounds and spoon over the warm strawberries and juice. Top with the second shortcake round and serve immediately cut into slices.

Carrot & Brazil Nut Traybake

Makes 18 squares

300g self-raising flour
350g caster sugar
2 teaspoons baking powder
100g Brazil nuts, chopped
2 teaspoons ground cinnamon
1 teaspoon ground ginger
300ml sunflower oil
300g carrots, grated
4 eggs, beaten
1 teaspoon vanilla extract

For the topping
400g low-fat soft cheese
1 tablespoon clear honey
Chopped Brazil nuts, to decorate

1 Preheat the oven to 180°C/350°F/Gas mark 4. Grease and base line a 30 x 23cm square cake tin.

2 For the cake, put the flour, sugar, baking powder, Brazil nuts, cinnamon and ground ginger into a large bowl. Add the sunflower oil, grated carrots, eggs and vanilla extract and beat together to mix well. Pour the mixture evenly into the prepared tin.

3 Bake in the oven for about 50 minutes, or until firm to the touch. Cool in the tin for 5-10 minutes, then turn out onto a wire rack and leave to cool completely.

4 For the topping, combine the soft cheese and honey in a bowl. Spread the topping mixture evenly over the top of the cake. Decorate with chopped Brazil nuts and serve in squares.

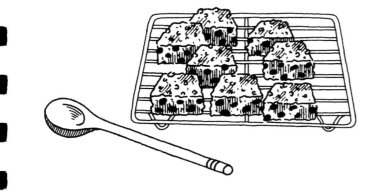

Valentine Cake

Makes 16 slices

225g soft margarine
225g golden caster sugar
4 eggs, beaten
200g self-raising flour
25g unsweetened cocoa powder, sifted
100g plain chocolate, melted

For the topping & icing
175g soft margarine
350g icing sugar, sifted
4 tablespoons unsweetened cocoa
    powder, sifted
750g poppy-red ready-to-roll
    fondant icing
Sugar roses and ribbon, to decorate

1 Preheat the oven to 180°C/350°F/Gas mark 4. Grease and base line a 26 x 26cm heart-shaped tin.

2 For the cake, beat the margarine and sugar together in a large bowl until pale and fluffy. Add the eggs, flour, cocoa powder and melted chocolate and beat together until smooth and well combined. Spoon the mixture into the prepared tin and level the surface.

3 Bake in the oven for 35–40 minutes, or until a skewer inserted into the centre comes out clean. Cool in the tin for 5 minutes, then turn out onto a wire rack and leave to cool completely.

4 Meanwhile, to make the topping, cream the margarine and one-third of the icing sugar together in a bowl. Gradually beat in the remaining icing sugar and the cocoa powder, mixing well.

5 Spread the chocolate icing evenly over the top and sides of the cake. Roll out the red fondant icing and use it to cover the cake. Decorate as desired with sugar roses and ribbon. Leave to set, then serve in slices.

Iced Sponge Cake

Makes 8–10 slices

250g plain flour
2 teaspoons baking powder
½ teaspoon salt
100g unsalted butter, softened
200g caster sugar
3 large eggs, beaten
1½ teaspoons vanilla extract
175ml milk

For the icing
4 egg whites
Pinch of cream of tartar
100g caster sugar
2 tablespoons chopped ready-to-eat
   dried apricots
2 tablespoons sultanas
2 tablespoons flaked almonds

1 Preheat the oven to 180°C/350°F/Gas mark 4. Grease and base line a 23cm round cake tin.

2 For the cake, sift the flour, baking powder and salt into a bowl. Set aside. In a separate bowl, cream the butter and sugar together until pale and fluffy. Gradually add the eggs, beating well after each addition, then beat in the vanilla extract. Fold in the flour mixture alternately with the milk and mix well.

3 Spoon the mixture into the prepared tin and level the surface. Bake in the oven for 30–40 minutes, or until pale golden and a skewer inserted into the centre comes out clean. Cool in the tin for 5 minutes, then turn out onto a wire rack and leave to cool completely.

4 Meanwhile, to make the icing, whisk the egg whites and cream of tartar together in a bowl until stiff peaks form. Gradually whisk in the sugar until the mixture is stiff and glossy.

5 Place the cake on an ovenproof serving plate. Swirl the icing evenly over the top of the cake, then sprinkle the top with the apricots, sultanas and almonds. Return the cake to a warm oven for 4–5 minutes to give the icing a little colour. Remove from the oven and set aside to cool. Serve in slices and eat on the day of making.

MUFFINS

- Blueberry Muffins
- Date Bran Muffins
- Wholemeal Banana & Walnut Muffins
- Pear & Walnut Muffins with Butterscotch Sauce
- Muesli-Topped Apple Sauce Muffins
- Peanut Butter Muffins
- Apple Streusel Muffins
- Red & Orange Muffins
- Clementine Muffins
- Ginger Rhubarb Muffins with Crème Anglaise
- Raspberry Cheesecake Muffins
- Apricot, Vanilla & Lemon Muffins
- Plum & Marzipan Muffins
- Sour Cherry Muffins Filled with Jam
- Moist Almond & Pear Muffins
- Cottage Cheese & Raisin Muffins

- Spiced Carrot Muffins with Soft Cheese
- Peach Upside-Down Muffins
- Caramel Orange Muffins
- Honey & Pistachio Muffins
- Vanilla Chocolate Chip Muffins
- Marshmallow, Choc & Cola Muffins
- Chocolate Chip Crumble Muffins
- Rich Chocolate Truffle Mini Muffins
- Dark Chocolate & Ginger Muffins
- Banana, Walnut & Choc-Chip Muffins
- Mint Chocolate Muffins
- White Chocolate & Macadamia Nut Muffins
- Chocolate & Brandy Dessert Muffins
- Chocolate Cheesecake Muffins
- Chocolate Fudge Muffins

- Chocolate-Filled Muffins
- Triple Chocolate Chunk Muffins
- Coffee Walnut Muffins
- Jam-Filled Mini Muffins
- Butter Tart Muffins with Raisins & Walnuts
- Gluten-Free Apple, Date & Walnut Muffins
- Cheese & Sun-Dried Tomato Muffins
- Bacon & Creamy Corn Muffins
- Fresh Tomato & Mixed Olive Muffins
- Plantain & Herb Muffins
- Beer & Onion Muffins
- Sweet Potato, Roasted Chilli & Feta Muffins
- Pizza Muffins
- Smoked Bacon & Blue Cheese Muffins

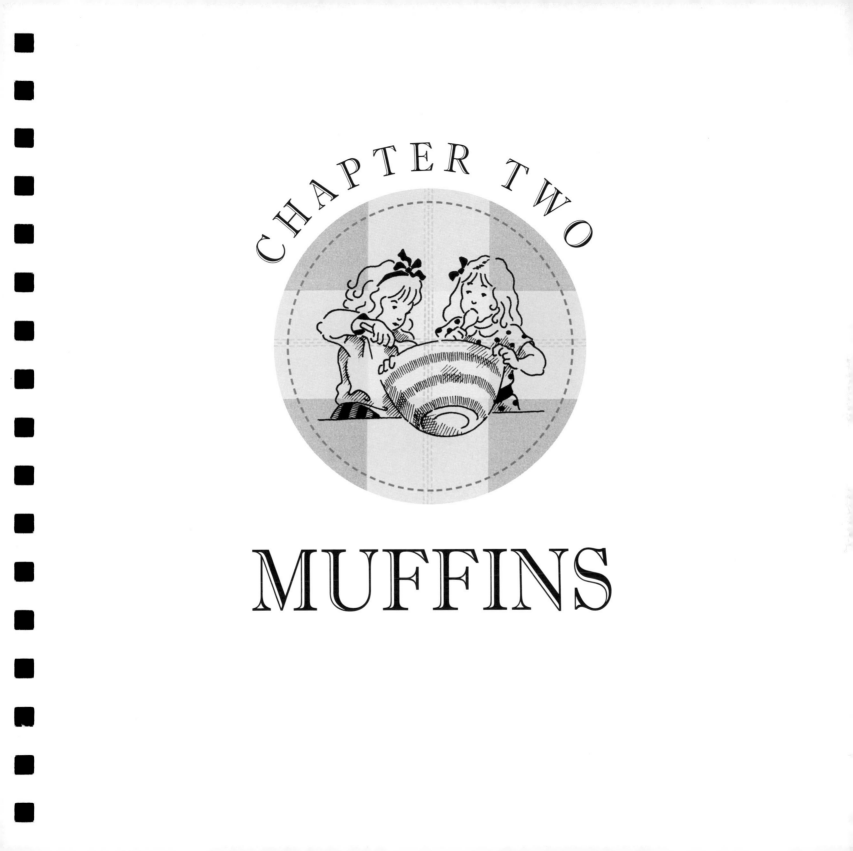

CHAPTER TWO

MUFFINS

Blueberry Muffins

Makes 12

300g self-raising flour
1 teaspoon baking powder
50g cold unsalted butter, cut
    into pieces
80g caster sugar
150g fresh blueberries
2 eggs, lightly beaten
225ml milk
1 teaspoon vanilla extract

Tip

Try using fresh
raspberries instead of the
blueberries, and replace the
vanilla extract with 1 teaspoon
ground mixed spice or
ground cinnamon,
if you like.

1 Preheat the oven to 200°C/400°F/Gas mark 6. Grease a 12-cup muffin tin or line the cups with paper muffin cases.

2 Mix the flour and baking powder together in a large bowl. Rub in the butter until the mixture resembles fine breadcrumbs. Stir the sugar and blueberries into this mixture.

3 In a separate small bowl or jug, mix the eggs, milk and vanilla extract together. Pour the egg mixture all at once into the dry ingredients and mix briefly until just combined.

4 Spoon the batter into the prepared muffin cups, dividing it evenly. Bake in the oven for about 20 minutes, or until risen and golden. Cool in the tin for 10 minutes, then turn out onto a wire rack. Serve warm or cold.

Date Bran Muffins

Makes 12

300g plain flour
1 teaspoon bicarbonate of soda
1 teaspoon ground cinnamon
125g caster sugar
80g wheat bran
120g stoned dried or fresh dates, finely
  chopped
125ml buttermilk
175ml milk
3 tablespoons sunflower oil
1 egg, lightly beaten

1 Mix the flour, bicarbonate of soda, cinnamon and sugar together in a large bowl. Add the wheat bran and dates and mix well.

2 In a separate small bowl, mix the buttermilk, milk, sunflower oil and egg together. Add the egg mixture all at once to the dry ingredients and mix briefly until just combined. Cover and refrigerate overnight.

3 The next day, preheat the oven to 200°C/400°F/Gas mark 6. Grease a 12-cup muffin tin or line the cups with paper muffin cases.

4 Remove the batter from the refrigerator and spoon it into the prepared muffin cups, dividing it evenly. Bake in the oven for about 20 minutes, or until risen and golden. Cool in the tin for 10 minutes, then turn out onto a wire rack. Serve warm or cold.

Wholemeal Banana
& Walnut Muffins

Makes 12

150g self-raising wholemeal flour
150g self-raising white flour
2 tablespoons soft light brown sugar
65g walnuts, chopped
3 large very ripe bananas, peeled
3 tablespoons sunflower oil
2 eggs, lightly beaten
5 tablespoons soured cream
2 tablespoons clear honey

1 Preheat the oven to 200°C/400°F/Gas mark 6. Grease a 12-cup muffin tin or line the cups with paper muffin cases.

2 Mix the flours, sugar and walnuts together in a large bowl. In a separate bowl, mash the bananas until fairly smooth using a potato masher or fork, then stir in the sunflower oil, eggs, soured cream and honey.

3 Add the wet ingredients all at once to the dry ingredients and mix briefly until just combined. Spoon the batter into the prepared muffin cups, dividing it evenly.

4 Bake in the oven for about 20 minutes, or until risen and golden. Cool in the tin for 10 minutes, then turn out onto a wire rack. Serve warm or cold.

Pear & Walnut Muffins

with Butterscotch Sauce

Makes 12

300g plain flour
2 teaspoons baking powder
½ teaspoon bicarbonate of soda
225g caster sugar
¼ teaspoon salt
1 teaspoon ground cinnamon
1 teaspoon ground cardamom
2 eggs, lightly beaten
175ml soured cream
175g unsalted butter, melted
3 canned pear halves in fruit juice,
   drained and diced
65g walnuts, coarsely chopped

For the butterscotch sauce
200g soft dark brown sugar
125g unsalted butter, cut into
   small pieces
4 tablespoons whipping cream

1 Preheat the oven to 200°C/400°F/Gas mark 6.
Grease a 12-cup muffin tin or line the cups
with paper muffin cases.

2 For the muffins, mix the flour, baking powder,
bicarbonate of soda, sugar, salt, cinnamon and
cardamom together in a large bowl.

3 In a separate bowl or jug, whisk the eggs,
soured cream and melted butter together.
Add the wet ingredients all at once to the dry
ingredients together with the pears and walnuts
and mix briefly until just combined.

4 Spoon the batter into the prepared muffin
cups, dividing it evenly. Bake in the oven for
about 20 minutes, or until risen and golden.

5 Meanwhile, for the butterscotch sauce,
combine the sugar and butter in a saucepan
and place over a low heat until the butter
has melted and sugar has dissolved, stirring
occasionally; do not allow the mixture to boil.
Remove the pan from the heat and add the
cream. Mix well and keep warm.

6 When the muffins are baked, cool them in the
tin for 10 minutes, then turn out onto a wire
rack. Serve warm, drizzled with the sauce.

Muesli-Topped
Apple Sauce Muffins

Makes 12

300g plain flour
100g soft light brown sugar
1 tablespoon baking powder
½ teaspoon bicarbonate of soda
½ teaspoon salt
½ teaspoon ground cinnamon
½ teaspoon freshly grated nutmeg
50g unsalted butter, melted
300g ready-made apple sauce
50ml milk
1 egg, lightly beaten
75g unsweetened muesli

Tip

Use a muesli with raisins or other dried fruit and nuts for added crunch and sweetness, but make sure that it is unsweetened.

1 Preheat the oven to 220°C/425°F/Gas mark 7. Grease a 12-cup muffin tin or line the cups with paper muffin cases.

2 Mix the flour, sugar, baking powder, bicarbonate of soda, salt, cinnamon and nutmeg together in a large bowl. In a separate bowl or jug, mix the melted butter, apple sauce, milk and egg together. Add the wet ingredients all at once to the dry ingredients and mix briefly until just combined. Spoon the batter into the prepared muffin cups, dividing it evenly.

3 Put the muesli into a bowl and crush lightly, using the back of a spoon or the end of a rolling pin, until the pieces are small and even. Sprinkle evenly over the muffins.

4 Bake in the oven for 15–20 minutes, or until risen and golden. Cool in the tin for 10 minutes, then turn out onto a wire rack. Serve warm or cold.

Peanut Butter Muffins

Makes 12

300g plain flour
1½ teaspoons baking powder
½ teaspoon salt
4 tablespoons finely chopped unsalted,
   roasted peanuts
100g soft light brown sugar
200g smooth peanut butter
175ml milk
2 tablespoons vegetable oil
2 eggs, lightly beaten
1 tablespoon demerara sugar

1 Preheat the oven to 190°C/375°F/Gas mark 5. Grease a 12-cup muffin tin or line the cups with paper muffin cases.

2 Mix the flour, baking powder and salt together in a large bowl. Stir in 2 tablespoons of the chopped peanuts and the soft brown sugar. Add the peanut butter and rub in until the mixture resembles coarse breadcrumbs.

3 In a separate bowl or jug, mix the milk, vegetable oil and eggs together. Add the wet ingredients all at once to the dry ingredients and mix briefly until just combined.

4 Spoon the batter into the prepared muffin cups, dividing it evenly. Combine the remaining chopped peanuts and demerara sugar, then sprinkle evenly over the tops of the muffins.

5 Bake in the oven for 16–18 minutes, or until risen and golden. Cool in the tin for 10 minutes, then turn out onto a wire rack. Serve warm or cold.

Apple Streusel Muffins

Makes 12

250g plain flour
2½ teaspoons baking powder
1½ teaspoons ground cinnamon
1 teaspoon ground ginger
Pinch of freshly grated nutmeg
½ teaspoon salt
150g caster sugar
1 egg, lightly beaten
150ml milk
6 tablespoons vegetable oil
50g sultanas
3 medium eating apples (about 225g
  total/unprepared weight),
  peeled, cored and chopped

For the topping
50g plain flour
40g cold unsalted butter, cut
  into small pieces
2 tablespoons soft light brown sugar

1 Preheat the oven to 190°C/375°F/Gas mark 5. Grease a 12-cup muffin tin or line the cups with paper muffin cases.

2 For the topping, sift the flour into a bowl. Rub the butter into the flour until the mixture resembles fine breadcrumbs. Stir in the sugar, then gather the dough together and gently squeeze it into a ball. Coarsely grate the dough and set aside.

3 For the muffins, mix the flour, baking powder, cinnamon, ginger, nutmeg, salt and sugar together in a large bowl. In a separate bowl, mix the egg, milk, vegetable oil, sultanas and apples together. Add the apple mixture all at once to the dry ingredients and mix briefly until just combined.

4 Spoon the batter into the prepared muffin cups, dividing it evenly, then sprinkle the tops with the grated topping. Bake in the oven for about 20 minutes, or until risen and golden. Cool in the tin for 10 minutes, then turn out onto a wire rack. Serve warm or cold.

Red & Orange Muffins

Makes 12

300g plain flour
225g caster sugar
1 tablespoon baking powder
½ teaspoon salt
125g fresh or frozen cranberries
   (thawed if frozen), coarsely chopped
Finely grated zest of 1 orange
2 tablespoons chopped pecan nuts
1 egg, lightly beaten
225ml milk
40g unsalted butter, melted

1 Preheat the oven to 200°C/400°F/Gas mark 6. Grease a 12-cup muffin tin or line the cups with paper muffin cases.

2 Mix the flour, sugar, baking powder and salt together in a large bowl. Stir in the cranberries, orange zest and pecan nuts.

3 In a separate bowl or jug, mix the egg, milk and melted butter together. Add the wet ingredients to the dry ingredients and mix briefly until just combined.

4 Spoon the batter into the prepared muffin cups, dividing it evenly. Bake in the oven for about 20 minutes, or until risen and golden. Cool in the tin for 10 minutes, then turn out onto a wire rack. Serve warm or cold.

Tip
Using fresh blueberries instead of the cranberries and walnuts instead of the pecan nuts would also work well in this recipe.

Clementine Muffins

Makes 12

300g plain flour
2 teaspoons baking powder
½ teaspoon salt
¼ teaspoon ground allspice
¼ teaspoon freshly grated nutmeg
125g caster sugar
60g cold margarine or unsalted butter,
    cut into small pieces
1 egg, lightly beaten
200ml milk
3 clementines or mandarin oranges,
    peeled, cut into segments and
    chopped

For the topping (optional)
65g caster sugar
½ teaspoon ground cinnamon
50g unsalted butter, melted

1 Preheat the oven to 180°C/350°F/Gas mark 4. Grease a 12-cup muffin tin or line the cups with paper muffin cases.

2 For the muffins, mix the flour, baking powder, salt, allspice, nutmeg and sugar together in a large bowl. Rub in the margarine or butter until the mixture resembles fine breadcrumbs.

3 In a separate bowl or jug, mix the egg and milk together. Pour the egg mixture all at once into the dry ingredients and mix briefly until just combined, then gently fold in the clementine or mandarin pieces.

4 Spoon the batter into the prepared muffin cups, dividing it evenly. Bake in the oven for 20–25 minutes, or until risen and golden.

5 Meanwhile, for the topping, if using, mix the sugar and cinnamon together in a small bowl and set aside. Remove the baked muffins from the tin while still warm. Dip the tops of the muffins in the melted butter, then dip in the cinnamon sugar. Transfer to a wire rack and cool for 10 minutes before serving.

Ginger Rhubarb Muffins
with Crème Anglaise

Makes 10

300g self-raising flour
2 teaspoons ground ginger
½ teaspoon baking powder
½ teaspoon bicarbonate of soda
¼ teaspoon salt
140g caster sugar
150g fresh rhubarb, finely chopped
1 egg, lightly beaten
150ml milk
150ml soured cream
4 tablespoons vegetable oil
1 tablespoon demerara sugar

For the Crème Anglaise
300ml milk
1 vanilla pod, split lengthways
3 egg yolks
1 teaspoon cornflour
1 tablespoon caster sugar

1 Preheat the oven to 190°C/375°F/Gas mark 5. Grease 10 cups of a 12-cup muffin tin or line 10 cups with paper muffin cases. For the Crème Anglaise, pour the milk into a heavy-based saucepan, add the vanilla pod and heat to boiling point. Turn off the heat and leave to infuse for about 15 minutes.

2 For the muffins, mix the flour, ginger, baking powder, bicarbonate of soda, salt and caster sugar together in a large bowl. Stir in the rhubarb. In a separate bowl, mix the egg, milk, soured cream and vegetable oil together. Add the wet ingredients all at once to the dry ingredients and mix briefly until just combined.

3 Spoon the batter into the prepared muffin cups, dividing it evenly, then sprinkle evenly with the demerara sugar. Bake in the oven for 18–20 minutes, or until well risen and golden. Cool in the tin for 5 minutes, then turn out onto a wire rack.

4 While the muffins are baking, finish the Crème Anglaise. Whisk the egg yolks, cornflour and sugar together in a heat-proof bowl until pale and creamy. Remove the vanilla pod from the milk and scrape out the seeds into the egg mixture. Reheat the milk to boiling point, then slowly pour into the egg mixture, whisking continuously. Pour back into the pan. Cook over a very low heat, stirring continuously for 10–15 minutes, or until the mixture thickens enough to coat the back of the spoon; do not allow the mixture to boil. Serve the muffins warm with the Crème Anglaise.

Raspberry Cheesecake
Muffins

Makes 12

225ml milk
75g cold unsalted butter,
   cut into pieces
1 teaspoon vanilla extract
2 eggs, lightly beaten
225g plain flour
125g caster sugar
2 teaspoons baking powder
½ teaspoon salt
100g fresh or frozen raspberries

For the cheesecake mixture
150g cream cheese or full-fat soft
   cheese, softened
160g caster sugar
1 egg
½ teaspoon vanilla extract

1 Preheat the oven to 200°C/400°F/Gas mark 6. Grease a 12-cup muffin tin or line the cups with paper muffin cases.

2 For the cheesecake mixture, mix the cream cheese or soft cheese, sugar, egg and vanilla extract together in a bowl. Set aside.

3 For the muffins, put the milk, butter and vanilla extract into a saucepan and heat gently, stirring, until the butter is melted. Remove the pan from the heat and allow to cool. Beat in the eggs.

4 Mix the flour, sugar, baking powder and salt together in a large bowl. Pour the milk mixture into the dry ingredients and mix briefly until just combined. Gently fold in the raspberries.

5 Spoon the batter into the prepared muffin cups, dividing it evenly. Top each muffin with 2 teaspoons of the cheese mixture and swirl slightly with a knife. Bake in the oven for about 20 minutes, or until the tops spring back when lightly pressed. Cool in the tin for 10 minutes, then turn out onto a wire rack. Serve warm or cold.

Apricot, Vanilla & Lemon
Muffins

Makes 12

½ vanilla pod
225g caster sugar
300g plain flour
1 tablespoon baking powder
¾ teaspoon salt
125g cold unsalted butter, cut
  into small pieces
100g ready-to-eat dried apricots,
  chopped
Finely grated zest of 1 lemon
1 egg, lightly beaten
225ml milk

Tip
If you don't have a vanilla pod, add 1 teaspoon of good-quality vanilla extract to the wet ingredients and add the sugar to the dry ingredients.

1 Preheat the oven to 200°C/400°F/Gas mark 6. Grease a 12-cup muffin tin or line the cups with paper muffin cases.

2 Put the vanilla pod and sugar into a food processor and process until the vanilla pod is very finely chopped. Mix the flour, baking powder and salt together in a large bowl, then stir in the vanilla sugar. Rub in the butter until the mixture resembles fine breadcrumbs. Stir in the dried apricots and lemon zest.

3 In a separate small bowl or jug, mix the egg and milk together. Pour the egg mixture all at once into the flour mixture, and mix briefly until just combined.

4 Spoon the batter into the prepared muffin cups, dividing it evenly. Bake in the oven for about 20 minutes, or until risen and golden. Cool in the tin for 10 minutes, then turn out onto a wire rack. Serve warm or cold.

Plum & Marzipan
Muffins

Makes 12

150g plain white flour
150g plain wholemeal flour
100g rolled oats
4 teaspoons baking powder
¾ teaspoon salt
50g wheat bran
150g soft light brown sugar
250g unpeeled stoned plums, chopped
175ml unsweetened orange juice
125ml vegetable oil
2 eggs, lightly beaten
Finely grated zest of ½ orange
100g marzipan, cut into small pieces
25g flaked almonds

1 Preheat the oven to 180°C/350°F/Gas mark 4. Grease a 12-cup muffin tin or line the cups with paper muffin cases.

2 Mix the flours, oats, baking powder, salt, wheat bran and sugar together in a large bowl. In a separate bowl or jug, mix the plums, orange juice, vegetable oil, eggs and orange zest together.

3 Add the wet ingredients all at once to the dry ingredients together with the marzipan and flaked almonds and mix briefly until just combined.

4 Spoon the batter into the prepared muffin cups, dividing it evenly. Bake in the oven for 25–30 minutes, or until risen and golden. Cool in the tin for 10 minutes, then turn out onto a wire rack. Serve warm or cold.

Sour Cherry Muffins
Filled with Jam

Makes 12

300g plain flour
1 teaspoon baking powder
½ teaspoon bicarbonate of soda
½ teaspoon salt
½ teaspoon ground cardamom
125g caster sugar
150g fresh cherries, stoned and
    coarsely chopped
50g unsalted butter, melted
1 egg, lightly beaten
225ml soured cream
½ teaspoon vanilla extract
3–4 tablespoons sour cherry jam
3 tablespoons flaked almonds

1 Preheat the oven to 200°C/400°F/Gas mark 6. Grease a 12-cup muffin tin or line the cups with paper muffin cases.

2 Mix the flour, baking powder, bicarbonate of soda, salt and cardamom together in a large bowl. Stir in the sugar and cherries and mix well.

3 In a separate bowl, beat the melted butter, egg, soured cream and vanilla extract together. Pour the egg mixture all at once into the flour mixture and mix briefly until just combined.

4 Spoon half of the batter evenly into the prepared muffin cups. Add about 1 teaspoon of jam to each muffin cup, then top with the remaining batter, dividing it evenly. Sprinkle the tops with the flaked almonds.

5 Bake in the oven for about 20 minutes, or until risen and golden. Cool in the tin for 10 minutes, then turn out onto a wire rack. Serve warm or cold.

Moist Almond & Pear
Muffins

Makes 12

300g plain flour
1 tablespoon baking powder
¼ teaspoon freshly grated nutmeg
4 tablespoons ground almonds
100g blanched almonds, chopped
100g marzipan, cut into small pieces
150g soft light brown sugar
1 egg, lightly beaten
200ml unsweetened pear or apple juice
75g unsalted butter, melted
2 small ripe pears, peeled, cored and
  chopped
25g flaked almonds
Sifted icing sugar, for dusting

Tip
If available, use
toasted blanched
almonds for a
more distinctive
nutty flavour.

1 Preheat the oven to 190°C/375°F/Gas mark 5. Grease a 12-cup muffin tin or line the cups with paper muffin cases.

2 Mix the flour, baking powder, nutmeg, ground and chopped almonds, marzipan and brown sugar together in a large bowl. In a separate bowl or jug, mix the egg, pear or apple juice, melted butter and pears together. Add the pear mixture all at once to the dry ingredients and mix briefly until just combined.

3 Spoon the batter into the prepared muffin cups, dividing it evenly, then sprinkle the tops with the flaked almonds. Bake in the oven for 18–20 minutes, or until well risen and golden.

4 Cool in the tin for 5 minutes, then turn out onto a wire rack. Dust the tops with sifted icing sugar and serve warm or cold.

Cottage Cheese & Raisin
Muffins

Makes 12

300g plain flour
375g toasted bran sticks, such as
   All-Bran cereal
175g caster sugar
1 tablespoon baking powder
½ teaspoon bicarbonate of soda
1 teaspoon ground cinnamon
1 teaspoon finely grated orange zest
½ teaspoon salt
250g cottage cheese
225ml natural yoghurt
2 tablespoons clear honey
50g unsalted butter, melted
2 eggs, lightly beaten
100g peeled carrots, grated
75g raisins

For the topping
2 tablespoons granulated sugar
1 teaspoon ground cinnamon

1 Preheat the oven to 200°C/400°F/Gas mark 6. Grease a 12-cup muffin tin or line the cups with paper muffin cases.

2 Mix the flour, toasted bran sticks, sugar, baking powder, bicarbonate of soda, cinnamon, orange zest and salt together in a large bowl.

3 In a separate bowl, mix the cottage cheese, yoghurt, honey, melted butter and eggs together. Add the wet ingredients all at once to the dry ingredients and mix briefly until just combined. Fold in the carrots and raisins.

4 Spoon the batter into the prepared muffin cups, dividing it evenly. Combine the sugar and cinnamon for the topping, then sprinkle this mixture over the tops of the muffins. Bake in the oven for 20–25 minutes, or until risen and golden. Cool in the tin for 10 minutes, then turn out onto a wire rack. Serve warm or cold.

Spiced Carrot Muffins
with Soft Cheese

Makes 12

300g plain flour
225g caster sugar
2 teaspoons bicarbonate of soda
2 teaspoons ground cinnamon
1 teaspoon salt
175ml vegetable oil
175ml milk
3 eggs, lightly beaten
100g peeled carrots, grated
120g walnuts, chopped
150g raisins

For the topping
85g cream cheese or full-fat soft
   cheese, softened
40g unsalted butter, softened
125g icing sugar, sifted
½ teaspoon vanilla extract

1 Preheat the oven to 180°C/350°F/Gas mark 4. Grease a 12-cup muffin tin or line the cups with paper muffin cases.

2 For the muffins, mix the flour, sugar, bicarbonate of soda, cinnamon and salt together in a large bowl. In a separate bowl or jug, mix the vegetable oil, milk and eggs together. Add the wet ingredients all at once to the dry ingredients together with the grated carrots, walnuts and raisins. Mix briefly until just combined.

3 Spoon the batter into the prepared muffin cups, dividing it evenly. Bake in the oven for 20–25 minutes, or until risen and golden. Cool in the tin for 10 minutes, then turn out onto a wire rack and leave to cool completely.

4 For the topping, beat the cream cheese or soft cheese and butter together in a bowl until light and fluffy. Beat in the icing sugar and vanilla extract until the topping is thick and spreadable. Spread a large tablespoonful of the topping mixture on top of each muffin before serving.

Peach Upside-Down
Muffins

Makes 12

60g cold unsalted butter, cut into 12
    pieces
100g soft light brown sugar
400g tin peach slices in fruit juice,
    drained
200g plain flour
225g caster sugar
2 teaspoons baking powder
½ teaspoon salt
2 eggs, lightly beaten
150ml soured cream
25g white vegetable margarine, melted

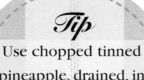

Tip
Use chopped tinned
pineapple, drained, in
place of peach slices,
if you prefer.

1 Preheat the oven to 190°C/375°F/Gas mark 5.
Grease a 12-cup non-stick muffin tin.

2 Divide the butter and brown sugar evenly
between the cups of the prepared tin. Place in
the oven for about 5 minutes, or until the butter
and sugar have melted. Remove from the oven and
arrange the peach slices in the bottoms of the
muffin cups.

3 Meanwhile, mix the flour, caster sugar, baking
powder and salt together in a large bowl. In a
separate bowl, mix the eggs, soured cream and
melted margarine together. Add the wet ingredients
all at once to the dry ingredients and mix briefly
until just combined.

4 Spoon the batter on top of the peach slices in
the muffin cups, dividing it evenly. Bake in the
oven for 20–25 minutes, or until risen and golden.
Cool in the tin for about 10 minutes, then invert the
muffins onto a plate or platter. Serve warm.

Caramel Orange Muffins

Makes 12

1 large orange, peeled
125g granulated sugar
340g self-raising flour
1 teaspoon baking powder
½ teaspoon ground cinnamon
¼ teaspoon ground cloves
¼ teaspoon ground allspice
Pinch of salt
50g cold unsalted butter, cut
 into small pieces
80g caster sugar
65g pistachio nuts, chopped
2 eggs, lightly beaten
225ml milk

1 Preheat the oven to 200°C/400°F/Gas mark 6. Grease a 12-cup muffin tin or line the cups with paper muffin cases.

2 Working over a bowl to collect any juice, cut the orange into segments, then coarsely chop them and add to the bowl. Set aside.

3 Combine the granulated sugar and 2 tablespoons of water in a small, heavy-based saucepan and stir over a low heat until the sugar has dissolved.

Increase the heat and bring the sugar mixture to the boil. Boil for about 7–10 minutes, or until the mixture has turned a dark caramel colour.

4 Remove the pan from the heat and carefully add the chopped orange flesh and all its juice. Be careful: the mixture will bubble fiercely. Leave the mixture to cool, then drain the oranges, reserving 175ml of the syrup.

5 Mix the flour, baking powder, cinnamon, cloves, allspice and salt together in a large bowl. Rub in the butter until the mixture resembles fine breadcrumbs, then stir in the caster sugar and pistachio nuts, mixing well.

6 In a separate small bowl or jug, mix the eggs and milk together, then pour into the dry ingredients. Add the drained oranges and mix until just combined. Spoon the batter into the muffin cups, dividing it evenly.

7 Bake in the oven for 18–20 minutes, or until well risen, golden and firm to the touch. Spoon the reserved orange caramel syrup over the hot muffins. Cool in the tin for 10 minutes, then turn out onto a wire rack. Serve warm.

Honey & Pistachio
Muffins

Makes 12

300g plain flour
1 tablespoon baking powder
½ teaspoon salt
1 teaspoon ground cinnamon
Pinch of ground cloves
3 tablespoons chopped pistachio nuts
3 tablespoons chopped blanched
    almonds
100g soft light brown sugar
4 tablespoons clear honey
225ml milk
2 tablespoons vegetable oil
2 eggs, lightly beaten

1 Preheat the oven to 200°C/400°F/Gas mark 6. Grease a 12-cup muffin tin or line the cups with paper muffin cases.

2 Mix the flour, baking powder, salt, cinnamon and cloves together in a large bowl. Stir in 2 tablespoons of the pistachio nuts, 2 tablespoons of the almonds and the sugar.

3 In a separate bowl or jug, mix 2 tablespoons of the honey, the milk, vegetable oil and eggs together. Add the wet ingredients all at once to the dry ingredients and mix briefly until just combined.

4 Spoon the batter into the prepared muffin cups, dividing it evenly, then sprinkle the tops with the remaining mixed chopped nuts.

5 Bake in the oven for 18–20 minutes, or until risen and golden. Drizzle the hot baked muffins with the remaining 2 tablespoons of honey. Cool in the tin for 10 minutes, then turn out onto a wire rack. These muffins are best eaten warm.

Vanilla Chocolate Chip
Muffins

Makes 12

300g self-raising flour
1 teaspoon baking powder
50g cold unsalted butter, cut into
    small pieces
80g caster sugar
150g milk or plain chocolate chips
2 eggs, lightly beaten
225ml milk
1 teaspoon vanilla extract

Tip

For chunkier chocolate chip muffins, measure 150g from a bar/block of milk or plain chocolate, then cut it into small chunks using a sharp knife and use the chopped chocolate instead of the chocolate chips.

1 Preheat the oven to 200°C/400°F/Gas mark 6. Grease a 12-cup muffin tin or line the cups with paper muffin cases.

2 Mix the flour and baking powder together in a large bowl. Rub in the butter until the mixture resembles fine breadcrumbs. Stir in the sugar and chocolate chips.

3 In a separate bowl or jug, mix the eggs, milk and vanilla extract together, then pour the egg mixture all at once into the dry ingredients and mix briefly until just combined.

4 Spoon the batter into the prepared muffin cups, dividing it evenly. Bake in the oven for 18–20 minutes, or until well risen, golden and firm to the touch. Cool in the tin for 10 minutes, then turn out onto a wire rack. Serve warm or cold.

Marshmallow, Choc
& Cola Muffins

Makes 12

250g self-raising flour
2 tablespoons unsweetened cocoa
    powder
1 teaspoon baking powder
Pinch of salt
125g caster sugar
1 egg, lightly beaten
6 tablespoons vegetable oil
150ml cola
75g mini marshmallows

Tip
If mini marshmallows
are not available, snip
larger marshmallows into
quarters using kitchen
scissors dipped in
icing sugar.

1 Preheat the oven to 190°C/375°F/Gas mark 5.
Grease a 12-cup muffin tin or line the cups with
paper muffin cases.

2 Mix the flour, cocoa powder, baking powder,
salt and sugar in a large bowl. In a separate
bowl or large jug, mix together the egg and
vegetable oil. Add the cola (it will froth up, so make
sure the container is large enough), then pour the
cola mixture all at once into the dry ingredients
and mix briefly until just combined.

3 Place a large spoonful of batter into each
prepared muffin cup, then add three or four
mini marshmallows, keeping them in the centre of
the muffin. Spoon the remaining batter on top,
dividing it evenly.

4 Bake in the oven for about 20 minutes, or until
well risen and firm to the touch. Cool in the tin
for 10 minutes, then turn out onto a wire rack.
Serve warm or cold.

Chocolate Chip Crumble
Muffins

Makes 12

250g self-raising flour
1 teaspoon baking powder
Pinch of salt
50g cold unsalted butter, cut into
  small pieces
100g soft light brown sugar
150g plain or milk chocolate chips
2 eggs, lightly beaten
225ml milk
2 teaspoons vanilla extract

For the topping
50g plain flour
1 tablespoon unsweetened
  cocoa powder
40g cold unsalted butter, cut
  into small pieces
2 tablespoons caster sugar

1 Preheat the oven to 200°C/400°F/Gas mark 6. Grease a 12-cup muffin tin or line the cups with paper muffin cases.

2 For the topping, sift the flour and cocoa powder into a bowl. Rub in the butter until the mixture resembles coarse breadcrumbs, then stir in the sugar. Set aside.

3 For the muffins, mix the flour, baking powder and salt together in a large bowl. Rub in the butter until the mixture resembles fine breadcrumbs. Stir in the sugar and chocolate chips.

4 In a separate bowl or jug, mix the eggs, milk and vanilla extract together. Pour the milk mixture all at once into the dry ingredients and mix briefly until just combined.

5 Spoon the batter into the prepared muffin cups, dividing it evenly, then sprinkle the tops with the crumble topping. Bake in the oven for 18–20 minutes, or until well risen and firm to the touch. Cool in the tin for 5 minutes, then turn out onto a wire rack. Serve warm or cold.

Rich Chocolate Truffle

Mini Muffins

Makes 24

125g self-raising flour
3 tablespoons unsweetened cocoa
   powder
¾ teaspoon baking powder
25g cold unsalted butter, cut
   into pieces
50g caster sugar
1 egg, lightly beaten
100ml milk
1 tablespoon double cream
1 teaspoon vanilla extract
Sifted icing sugar, for dusting

For the chocolate ganache
75g plain or milk chocolate chips
5 tablespoons double cream

1 Preheat the oven to 200°C/400°F/Gas mark 6. Grease two 12-cup mini muffin tins or one 24-cup mini muffin tin, or line the cups with paper mini muffin cases.

2 For the muffins, mix the flour, cocoa powder and baking powder together in a large bowl. Rub in the butter until the mixture resembles fine breadcrumbs. Stir in the caster sugar.

3 In a separate small bowl or jug, mix the egg, milk, cream and vanilla extract together, then pour the egg mixture all at once into the dry ingredients and mix briefly until just combined.

4 Spoon the batter into the prepared muffin cups, dividing it evenly. Bake in the oven for 8–10 minutes, or until well risen and firm to the touch. Cool in the tins for 5 minutes, then turn out onto a wire rack to cool completely.

5 While the muffins are baking, make the chocolate ganache. Put the chocolate chips in a small heat-proof bowl. Bring the cream to the boil in a small saucepan. Pour the hot cream over the chocolate chips and stir until melted and smooth. Leave for about 1 hour to cool and thicken.

6 When the ganache is the consistency of softened butter, beat it for a few seconds, then spread a swirl of ganache on top of each muffin. Lightly dust the muffins with sifted icing sugar before serving.

Dark Chocolate

& Ginger Muffins

Makes 10

200g plain chocolate, roughly chopped
75g cold unsalted butter, cut into
    small pieces
300g self-raising flour
150g soft light brown sugar
¾ teaspoon bicarbonate of soda
Pinch of salt
50g preserved stem ginger, drained
    and finely chopped, plus extra to
    decorate
175ml soured cream
3 tablespoons golden syrup
1 egg, lightly beaten
2 teaspoons vanilla extract
50g white chocolate, broken into
    squares

1 Preheat the oven to 200°C/400°F/Gas mark 6. Grease 10 cups of a 12-cup muffin tin or line 10 cups with paper muffin cases.

2 Melt the plain chocolate and butter together in a heat-proof bowl set over a pan of barely simmering water, stirring occasionally until smooth. Remove from the heat and cool for a few minutes.

3 Mix the flour, sugar, bicarbonate of soda, salt and stem ginger together in a large bowl. In a separate bowl or jug, mix the soured cream, golden syrup, egg and vanilla extract together, then add the melted chocolate mixture and stir until blended. Add the wet ingredients all at once to the dry ingredients and mix briefly until just combined.

4 Spoon the batter into the prepared muffin cups, dividing it evenly. Bake in the oven for about 20 minutes, or until risen and firm to the touch. Cool in the tin for 10 minutes, then turn out onto a wire rack to cool completely.

5 Melt the white chocolate in a small heat-proof bowl set over a pan of barely simmering water, stirring occasionally until smooth. Spoon the melted white chocolate into a small greaseproof paper piping bag, snip off the end and pipe zig-zags of chocolate over the tops of the muffins. Scatter a few pieces of chopped stem ginger over each and leave to set before serving.

Banana, Walnut
& Choc-Chip Muffins

Makes 12

300g self-raising flour
2 tablespoons soft light brown sugar
60g walnuts, chopped
100g plain chocolate chips
2 ripe bananas (about 250g total
    weight), peeled
3 tablespoons vegetable oil
2 eggs, lightly beaten
125ml soured cream

1 Preheat the oven to 200ºC/400ºF/Gas mark 6. Grease a 12-cup muffin tin or line the cups with paper muffin cases.

2 Mix the flour, sugar, walnuts and chocolate chips together in a large bowl. In a separate bowl, mash the bananas until fairly smooth, then stir in the vegetable oil, eggs and soured cream.

3 Add the wet ingredients all at once to the dry ingredients. Mix briefly until just combined.

4 Spoon the batter into the prepared muffin cups, dividing it evenly. Bake in the oven for about 20 minutes, or until risen and golden. Cool in the tin for 10 minutes, then turn out onto a wire rack. Serve warm or cold.

Mint Chocolate

Muffins

Makes 10

250g plain flour
2 tablespoons unsweetened cocoa
  powder
2 teaspoons baking powder
½ teaspoon bicarbonate of soda
100g soft light brown sugar
150g chocolate mints or mint-flavoured
  chocolate, roughly chopped
1 egg, separated
Pinch of salt
85g unsalted butter, melted
125ml soured cream
125ml milk

For the icing

125ml whipping cream
¼ teaspoon peppermint essence
1–2 drops green food colouring
4 tablespoons caster sugar
100g pistachio nuts, chopped

1 Preheat the oven to 200°C/400°F/Gas mark 6. Grease 10 cups of a 12-cup muffin tin or line 10 cups with paper muffin cases.

2 For the muffins, mix the flour, cocoa powder, baking powder, bicarbonate of soda, sugar and chocolate mints or mint-flavoured chocolate together in a large bowl.

3 Put the egg white and salt in a clean bowl and whisk until soft peaks form. In a separate bowl or jug, mix the egg yolk, melted butter, soured cream and milk together. Pour the milk mixture all at once into the dry ingredients and mix briefly until almost combined. Add the whisked egg white and gently fold into the mixture until combined.

4 Spoon the batter into the prepared muffin cups, dividing it evenly. Bake in the oven for 18–20 minutes, or until well risen and firm to the touch. Cool in the tin for 10 minutes, then turn out onto a wire rack to cool completely.

5 To make the icing, whip the cream in a bowl until soft peaks form. Add the peppermint essence and a drop or two of green food colouring, then whisk in the sugar a spoonful at a time until the mixture is fairly stiff. Spoon or pipe the icing on top of the muffins, then scatter over the pistachio nuts. Serve within 1 hour of icing.

White Chocolate
& Macadamia Nut Muffins

Makes 12

175g plain chocolate, coarsely chopped
or broken into squares
225g plain flour
150g soft light brown sugar
2 tablespoons unsweetened cocoa
powder
1 teaspoon baking powder
½ teaspoon salt
175ml buttermilk
2 eggs, lightly beaten
1½ teaspoons vanilla extract
200g white chocolate, chopped
100g unsalted macadamia
nuts, coarsely chopped

1 Preheat the oven to 200°C/400°F/Gas mark 6. Grease a 12-cup muffin tin or line the cups with paper muffin cases.

2 Melt the plain chocolate in a small heat-proof bowl set over a pan of barely simmering water, stirring occasionally until smooth. Remove from the heat and set aside.

3 Mix the flour, sugar, cocoa powder, baking powder and salt together in a large bowl. In a separate bowl or jug, mix the buttermilk, eggs and vanilla extract together.

4 Add the buttermilk mixture and the melted chocolate all at once to the dry ingredients and mix briefly until just combined. Fold in the white chocolate and macadamia nuts.

5 Spoon the batter into the prepared muffin cups, dividing it evenly. Bake in the oven for about 20 minutes, or until well risen and firm to the touch. Cool in the tin for 5 minutes, then turn out onto a wire rack. Serve warm or cold.

Chocolate & Brandy
Dessert Muffins

Makes 12

300g self-raising flour
1 teaspoon baking powder
50g unsweetened cocoa powder
225g caster sugar
1 egg, lightly beaten
175ml buttermilk
125g unsalted butter, melted
2 tablespoons brandy
Finely grated zest of 1 small orange
2 teaspoons icing sugar, sifted
Fresh fruit, to serve

For the white chocolate sauce

200g white chocolate, broken into
   squares
6 tablespoons double cream
4 tablespoons single cream

1 Preheat the oven to 190°C/375°F/Gas mark 5. Grease a 12-cup non-stick muffin tin.

2 For the muffins, mix the flour, baking powder, cocoa powder and caster sugar together in a large bowl. In a separate bowl or jug, mix the egg, buttermilk, melted butter, brandy and orange zest together. Add the wet ingredients all at once to the dry ingredients and mix briefly until just combined.

3 Spoon the batter into the prepared muffin cups, dividing it evenly. Bake in the oven for 18–20 minutes, or until well risen and firm to the touch. Cool in the tin for 5 minutes, then turn out onto a wire rack to cool completely.

4 For the white chocolate sauce, melt the chocolate and 2 tablespoons of the double cream in a heat-proof bowl set over a pan of barely boiling water, stirring occasionally until smooth. Add the remaining double cream and the single cream and stir until blended. Remove from the heat and whisk the chocolate sauce until smooth.

5 Place a chocolate muffin on a plate and top with fresh fruit. Pour over a little of the warm white chocolate sauce, letting it dribble down the side. Repeat with the remaining muffins. Dust with sifted icing sugar before serving.

Chocolate Cheesecake
Muffins

Makes 12

150g plain flour
175g caster sugar
35g unsweetened cocoa powder
½ teaspoon bicarbonate of soda
¼ teaspoon salt
125ml soured cream
3 tablespoons vegetable oil
50g unsalted butter, melted
2 eggs, lightly beaten
1 teaspoon vanilla extract
75g plain chocolate, melted
25g almonds, chopped

For the cheesecake mixture
175g cream cheese or full-fat soft
    cheese, softened
60g caster sugar
1 egg, lightly beaten
⅛ teaspoon vanilla extract

1 Preheat the oven to 190°C/375°F/Gas mark 5. Grease a 12-cup muffin tin or line the cups with paper muffin cases.

2 For the cheesecake mixture, combine all the ingredients in a bowl and set aside.

3 For the muffins, mix the flour, sugar, cocoa powder, bicarbonate of soda and salt together in a large bowl. In a separate bowl or jug, mix the soured cream, vegetable oil, melted butter, eggs, vanilla extract and melted chocolate together. Add the wet ingredients all at once to the dry ingredients and mix briefly until just combined.

4 Spoon the batter into the prepared muffin cups, dividing it evenly, then carefully spoon a little of the cheesecake mixture over the chocolate batter in each muffin cup. Swirl the mixture slightly with a knife so that the batter appears marbled. Sprinkle the tops with the flaked almonds.

5 Bake in the oven for 20–25 minutes, or until risen and firm to the touch. Cool in the tin for 5 minutes, then turn out onto a wire rack. Serve warm or cold.

Chocolate Fudge Muffins

Makes 12

150g plain chocolate, coarsely chopped
50g dark bitter chocolate, coarsely
   chopped
75g unsalted butter, cut into
   small pieces
300g plain flour
150g soft light brown sugar
1 teaspoon bicarbonate of soda
¼ teaspoon salt
175ml soured cream
3 tablespoons golden syrup
1 egg, lightly beaten
1¼ teaspoons vanilla extract
100g plain chocolate chips

Tip

Dark bitter chocolate
with a cocoa solids content
of 70% (minimum)
would work well in
this recipe.

1 Preheat the oven to 200°C/400°F/Gas mark 6. Grease a 12-cup muffin tin or line the cups with paper muffin cases.

2 Melt the plain chocolate, bitter chocolate and butter together in a heat-proof bowl set over a pan of barely simmering water, stirring occasionally until smooth. Remove from the heat and cool slightly.

3 Mix the flour, sugar, bicarbonate of soda and salt, together in a large bowl. In a separate small bowl or jug, mix the soured cream, golden syrup, egg and vanilla extract, then fold this into the melted chocolate mixture together. Fold in the chocolate chips. Add the chocolate mixture all at once to the dry ingredients and mix briefly until just combined.

4 Spoon the batter into the prepared muffin cups, dividing it evenly. Bake in the oven for about 20 minutes, or until well risen and firm to the touch. Cool in the tin for 5 minutes, then turn out onto a wire rack. Serve warm or cold.

Chocolate-Filled Muffins

Makes 12

300g self-raising flour
1 teaspoon baking powder
50g cold unsalted butter, cut into
    small pieces
80g caster sugar
2 eggs, lightly beaten
225ml milk
1 teaspoon vanilla extract
2 tablespoons finely chopped
    hazelnuts
1 tablespoon demerara sugar

For the filling
20g unsalted butter, softened
75g icing sugar
1½ teaspoons milk
½ teaspoon vanilla extract
50g plain chocolate, melted

1 Preheat the oven to 200°C/400°F/Gas mark 6. Grease a 12-cup muffin tin or line the cups with paper muffin cases.

2 For the filling, beat the butter in a small bowl until creamy. Gradually add the icing sugar, beating until well mixed. Beat in the milk, vanilla extract and melted chocolate until well combined. Set aside.

3 For the muffins, mix the flour and baking powder in a large bowl. Rub in the butter until the mixture resembles fine breadcrumbs. Stir in the caster sugar. In a separate bowl or jug, mix the eggs, milk and vanilla extract together. Pour the egg mixture all at once into the dry ingredients and mix briefly until just combined.

4 Put a spoonful of the batter into each prepared muffin cup. Drop a large teaspoonful of the filling mixture on top of each, then cover with the remaining muffin batter, dividing it evenly.

5 Mix the chopped hazelnuts and demerara sugar together and sprinkle this mixture evenly over the tops of the muffins.

6 Bake in the oven for 18–20 minutes, or until well risen, golden and firm to the touch. Cool in the tin for 5 minutes, then turn out onto a wire rack. These muffins are best served warm.

Triple Chocolate Chunk
Muffins

Makes 10

250g plain flour
2 teaspoons baking powder
½ teaspoon bicarbonate of soda
100g soft light brown sugar
50g plain chocolate, roughly chopped
50g milk chocolate, roughly chopped
50g white chocolate, roughly chopped
1 egg, separated
¼ teaspoon salt
85g unsalted butter, melted
50ml soured cream
175ml milk
1 teaspoon vanilla extract

Tip
If you prefer, use just one or two types of chocolate. Flavoured chocolates, such as orange, mint or hazelnut varieties, would also work well.

1 Preheat the oven to 200°C/400°F/Gas mark 6. Grease 10 cups of a 12-cup muffin tin or line 10 cups with paper muffin cases.

2 Mix the flour, baking powder, bicarbonate of soda, sugar and about two-thirds of each type of chocolate together in a large bowl.

3 Put the egg white and salt into a clean bowl and whisk until soft peaks form. In a separate bowl or jug, mix the egg yolk, melted butter, soured cream, milk and vanilla extract together. Pour the milk mixture all at once into the dry ingredients and mix briefly until almost combined. Add the whisked egg white and gently fold into the mixture until combined.

4 Spoon the batter into the prepared muffin cups, dividing it evenly, then gently press the remaining mixed chocolate on top of the muffins. Bake in the oven for 18–20 minutes, or until well risen and firm to the touch. Cool in the tin for 10 minutes, then turn out onto a wire rack. Serve warm or cold.

Coffee Walnut Muffins

Makes 12

125g walnut halves
150g unsalted butter, cut into
    small pieces
150g granulated sugar
3 egg whites
4 egg yolks
1 teaspoon vanilla extract
150g plain flour
1 teaspoon baking powder

For the icing
1½ tablespoons milk
Small knob of unsalted butter
1 tablespoon instant coffee granules
200g icing sugar, sifted
1 teaspoon vanilla extract

1 Preheat the oven to 180°C/350°F/Gas mark 4.
Grease a 12-cup muffin tin or line the cups with
paper muffin cases.

2 Reserve 12 walnut halves for decoration, then
finely chop the remainder in a food processor.

3 Melt the butter and sugar in a heavy-based
saucepan over a low heat. Gently bring the

mixture to the boil and cook for 2 minutes, stirring
continuously. Be careful not to brown or burn the
mixture. Remove the pan from the heat and set
aside to cool.

4 Whisk the egg whites in a clean bowl until stiff
peaks form and set aside. Add the egg yolks to
the cooled sugar-butter mixture, then stir in the
chopped walnuts, vanilla extract, flour and baking
powder. Gently fold in the whisked egg whites to
make a soft, thick batter.

5 Spoon the batter into the prepared muffin
cups, dividing it evenly. Bake in the oven for
15–20 minutes, or until golden and firm to the
touch. Cool in the tin for 10 minutes, then turn out
onto a wire rack to cool completely.

6 For the icing, heat the milk, butter and coffee
in a small saucepan over a low heat, stirring
until the butter has melted. Add the icing sugar and
vanilla extract and stir until smooth and combined,
adding a little more icing sugar if necessary to make
a spreading consistency. Spread some icing on top
of each muffin and top with a walnut half. Leave to
set before serving.

Jam-Filled Mini Muffins

Makes 36

250g self-raising flour
1 teaspoon baking powder
50g cold unsalted butter, cut into
    small pieces
80g caster sugar
2 eggs, lightly beaten
225ml milk
1 teaspoon vanilla extract
5–6 tablespoons raspberry or
    strawberry jam

For the topping
50g unsalted butter, cut into
    small pieces
1 teaspoon ground cinnamon
50g granulated sugar

1 Preheat the oven to 200°C/400°F/Gas mark 6. Grease three 12-cup mini muffin tins or one 24-cup mini muffin tin and one 12-cup mini muffin tin, or line the cups with paper mini muffin cases.

2 For the muffins, mix the flour and baking powder together in a large bowl. Rub in the butter until the mixture resembles fine breadcrumbs. Stir in the sugar.

3 In a separate small bowl, mix the eggs, milk and vanilla extract together, then pour the egg mixture all at once into the dry ingredients and mix briefly until just combined.

4 Put a small spoonful of the mixture into each prepared muffin cup. Add about ½ teaspoon of jam to each, then top with the remaining muffin batter, dividing it evenly. Bake in the oven for 8–10 minutes, or until well risen, golden and firm to the touch. Cool in the tin for a few minutes, then turn out onto a wire rack.

5 For the topping, melt the butter in a small saucepan over a low heat, then remove the pan from the heat. In a small bowl, mix the cinnamon and sugar together. Brush each baked warm mini muffin all over with a little of the melted butter, then roll in the cinnamon sugar. Set aside to cool. Serve warm or cold.

Butter Tart Muffins
with Raisins & Walnuts

Makes 12

200g raisins
175g granulated sugar
125g unsalted butter, cut into small
    pieces
125ml milk
1 teaspoon vanilla or rum extract
2 eggs, lightly beaten
300g plain flour
2 teaspoons baking powder
1 teaspoon bicarbonate of soda
Pinch of salt
65g walnuts, chopped
3–4 tablespoons golden syrup

Tip

Try using sultanas or
chopped ready-to-eat dried
apricots instead of raisins,
and pecans or pine nuts
instead of walnuts.

1 Preheat the oven to 190°C/375°F/Gas mark 5. Grease a 12-cup muffin tin or line the cups with paper muffin cases.

2 Combine the raisins, sugar, butter, milk and vanilla or rum extract in a saucepan. Cook over a medium heat, stirring almost continuously, until hot and the sugar has melted. Bring just to a simmer, then remove the pan from the heat. Leave the mixture to cool for 10 minutes, then whisk in the eggs. Set aside to cool until just warm.

3 Mix the flour, baking powder, bicarbonate of soda and salt together in a large bowl. Make a well in the centre and pour in the raisin mixture, stirring briefly until just combined. Gently fold in the walnuts, then spoon the batter into the prepared muffin cups, dividing it evenly. Bake in the oven for 15–17 minutes, or until risen and golden.

4 Remove from the oven and immediately drizzle about 1 teaspoon of golden syrup over the top of each muffin. Cool in the tin for 10 minutes, then turn out onto a wire rack. Serve warm or cold.

Gluten-Free Apple, Date & Walnut Muffins

Makes 12

250g white or brown rice flour

50g soya flour

25g cornflour

1 tablespoon gluten-free baking powder

½ teaspoon salt

1 teaspoon ground cinnamon

½ teaspoon ground mixed spice

125g golden caster sugar

75g stoned dried dates, chopped

35g walnuts, chopped

2 eggs, lightly beaten

175ml milk

6 tablespoons sunflower oil

2 medium eating apples, peeled, cored and finely chopped

For the topping

65g walnuts, chopped

2 tablespoons golden caster sugar

1 Preheat the oven to 190°C/375°F/Gas mark 5. Grease a 12-cup muffin tin or line the cups with paper muffin cases.

2 For the muffins, sift the rice flour and soya flour, cornflour, baking powder, salt, cinnamon and mixed spice into a large bowl. Stir in the sugar, dates and walnuts. In a separate bowl, mix the eggs, milk, sunflower oil and apples together. Add the apple mixture all at once to the dry ingredients and mix briefly until just combined.

3 Spoon the batter into the prepared muffin cups, dividing it evenly. Mix the topping ingredients together in a small bowl, then sprinkle this mixture over the tops of the muffins.

4 Bake in the oven for about 20 minutes, or until risen and firm to the touch. Cool in the tin for 5 minutes, then turn out onto a wire rack. Serve warm or cold.

Tip
Unlike in other muffin recipes, the flours and other fine dry ingredients are sifted here to ensure that they are well-mixed and aerated.

Cheese & Sun-dried
Tomato Muffins

Makes 10

300g plain flour
1 tablespoon baking powder
1 tablespoon caster sugar
150g grated mozzarella or Cheddar
   cheese
5 tablespoons olive oil
2 eggs, lightly beaten
125ml milk
2 cloves garlic, crushed
75g sun-dried tomatoes (drained if in
   oil), chopped
50g pitted black olives, roughly
   chopped
2 teaspoons chopped fresh or
   1 teaspoon dried oregano
Salt and freshly ground black pepper,
   to taste

1 Preheat the oven to 190°C/375°F/Gas mark 5. Grease 10 cups of a 12-cup muffin tin or line 10 cups with paper muffin cases.

2 Mix the flour, baking powder, sugar and mozzarella or Cheddar cheese together in a large bowl. In a separate bowl or jug, mix the olive oil, eggs and milk together. Stir in the garlic, sun-dried tomatoes, olives, oregano and salt and pepper. Add the wet ingredients all at once to the dry ingredients and mix briefly until just combined.

3 Spoon the batter into the prepared muffin cups, dividing it evenly. Bake in the oven for about 20 minutes, or until well risen and firm to the touch. Cool in the tin for 5 minutes, then turn out onto a wire rack. Serve warm or cold.

Tip
If the sun-dried tomatoes aren't moist, soak them for about 10 minutes in the milk and oil mixture before adding to the dry ingredients.

Bacon & Creamy Corn
Muffins

Makes 12

225g rindless streaky bacon rashers
1 small onion, finely chopped
150g plain flour
170g cornmeal or instant polenta
2 tablespoons caster sugar
4 teaspoons baking powder
½ teaspoon salt
200g canned creamed sweetcorn
125ml milk
1 egg, lightly beaten

1 Preheat the oven to 200°C/400°F/Gas mark 6. Grease a 12-cup muffin tin or line the cups with paper muffin cases.

2 Cook the bacon in a large frying pan (or under a preheated grill) until crisp. Remove the bacon from the pan and drain well on kitchen paper. Add the onion to the same pan and sauté for about 5-7 minutes, or until soft and lightly golden. Remove the onion from the pan. Break or chop the bacon into small pieces and set aside with the onion. Reserve about 3 tablespoons of the bacon fat (or substitute vegetable oil).

3 Mix the flour, cornmeal or polenta, sugar, baking powder and salt together in a bowl. In a separate bowl or jug, beat the creamed sweetcorn, milk, egg and reserved bacon fat (or vegetable oil) together. Add the corn mixture all at once to the flour mixture and mix briefly until just combined. Fold in the reserved bacon and onion.

4 Spoon the batter into the prepared muffin cups, dividing it evenly. Bake in the oven for about 20 minutes, or until golden. Cool in the tin for 5 minutes, then carefully turn out onto a wire rack. These muffins are best served warm from the oven.

Fresh Tomato
& Mixed Olive Muffins

Makes 12

300g plain flour
1 tablespoon baking powder
1 tablespoon caster sugar
25g fresh Parmesan cheese, finely
  grated
3 tablespoons chopped fresh basil
1 egg, lightly beaten
175ml milk
100g unsalted butter, melted
1 tablespoon olive oil
4 medium ripe tomatoes, skinned,
  seeded and chopped
50g pitted mixed black and green
  olives, roughly chopped
1 clove garlic, crushed
Salt and freshly ground black pepper,
  to taste

For the topping
40g fresh white breadcrumbs
25g fresh Parmesan cheese, finely
  grated
2 teaspoons poppy seeds

1 Preheat the oven to 200°C/400°F/Gas mark 6. Grease a 12-cup muffin tin or line the cups with paper muffin cases.

2 For the muffins, mix the flour, baking powder, sugar, Parmesan cheese and basil together in a large bowl. In a separate bowl, mix the egg, milk, melted butter, olive oil, tomatoes, olives, garlic and salt and pepper together. Pour the tomato mixture all at once into the dry ingredients and mix briefly until just combined.

3 Spoon the batter into the prepared muffin cups, dividing it evenly. For the topping, mix all the ingredients together in a bowl. Sprinkle this mixture over the tops of the muffins.

4 Bake in the oven for about 20 minutes, or until well risen and lightly browned. Cool in the tin for 5 minutes, then turn out onto a wire rack. Serve warm or cold.

Plantain & Herb Muffins

Makes 12

300g plain flour
1 tablespoon baking powder
1 teaspoon bicarbonate of soda
1 teaspoon salt
1 tablespoon chopped fresh thyme
   leaves
1 tablespoon snipped fresh chives
1 tablespoon chopped fresh parsley
1 clove garlic, crushed
175ml natural yoghurt
150ml milk
2 eggs, lightly beaten
2 tablespoons vegetable oil
1 tablespoon horseradish sauce
1 large green plantain, peeled
   and grated

1 Preheat the oven to 200°C/400°F/Gas mark 6. Grease a 12-cup muffin tin or line the cups with paper muffin cases.

2 Mix the flour, baking powder, bicarbonate of soda and salt together in a large bowl. Add the thyme, chives, parsley and garlic and mix well.

3 In a separate bowl or jug, mix the yoghurt, milk, eggs and vegetable oil together. Add the wet ingredients all at once to the dry ingredients, together with the horseradish sauce and grated plantain, and mix briefly until just combined.

4 Spoon the batter into the prepared muffin cups, dividing it evenly. Bake in the oven for 20–25 minutes, or until risen and golden. Cool in the tin for 10 minutes, then turn out onto a wire rack. Serve warm or cold.

Tip
Plantains can be eaten at every stage of ripeness but must be cooked. When green, their flavour and texture is akin to potato; when ripe (and black), they are more similar to bananas.

Beer & Onion Muffins

Makes 12

300g plain flour
2 tablespoons caster sugar
1 tablespoon baking powder
1 teaspoon salt
$\frac{1}{2}$ teaspoon freshly ground black pepper
$\frac{1}{2}$ teaspoon garlic powder
225ml beer, allowed to go flat and at room temperature
125ml vegetable oil
1 egg, lightly beaten
1 small onion, grated
1 tablespoon chopped fresh thyme leaves

1 Preheat the oven to 200°C/400°F/Gas mark 6. Grease a 12-cup muffin tin or line the cups with paper muffin cases.

2 Mix the flour, sugar, baking powder, salt, pepper and garlic powder together in a large bowl.

3 In a separate bowl or jug, whisk the beer, vegetable oil, egg, onion and thyme together. Add the wet ingredients all at once to the dry ingredients and mix briefly until just combined.

4 Spoon the batter into the prepared muffin cups, dividing it evenly. Bake in the oven for 20–25 minutes, or until risen and golden. Cool in the tin for 10 minutes, then turn out onto a wire rack. Serve warm.

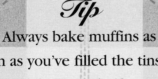

Tip
Always bake muffins as soon as you've filled the tins, on the middle oven shelf or just a little higher. Close the oven door as quickly as possible to prevent heat being lost.

Sweet Potato, Roasted
Chilli & Feta Muffins

Makes 12

1 medium orange-fleshed sweet potato
1 fresh hot red chilli
300g plain flour
1 tablespoon baking powder
½ teaspoon salt
1 clove garlic, crushed
1 teaspoon cumin seeds, toasted and
  lightly crushed
1 tablespoon chopped fresh basil
2 eggs, lightly beaten
225ml milk
3 tablespoons olive oil, plus extra
  for brushing
75g feta cheese, crumbled

1 Preheat the oven to 200°C/400°F/Gas mark 6. Grease a 12-cup muffin tin or line the cups with paper muffin cases.

2 Prick the sweet potato several times with a fork and place it on a small baking sheet or a piece of foil. Bake in the oven for 30–45 minutes, or until tender. Remove from the oven and set aside until cool enough to handle. Once cool, scoop out and mash the flesh. Set aside.

3 Brush the chilli with a little olive oil and place under a preheated grill or over a naked flame, turning frequently, until it is scorched and blackened all over. Put the hot chilli into a small plastic food bag and leave until cool enough to handle. Peel the chilli, removing all the blackened skin, then slit the chilli open lengthways and remove the stem, seeds and membranes. Finely chop the chilli flesh. Set aside.

4 Mix the flour, baking powder and salt together in a large bowl. Stir in the garlic, cumin and basil. In a separate bowl or jug, beat the eggs, milk, olive oil and mashed sweet potato together. Add the egg mixture all at once to the dry ingredients, together with the chopped chilli. Fold in the feta cheese and briefly mix until just combined.

5 Spoon the batter into the prepared muffin cups, dividing it evenly. Bake in the oven for 20–25 minutes, or until well risen and golden. Cool in the tin for 10 minutes, then turn out onto a wire rack. These muffins are best served warm.

Pizza Muffins

Makes 12

5 tablespoons olive oil
65g mushrooms, sliced
50g pepperoni, chopped
85g lean cooked ham, chopped
1 onion, grated
150g mozzarella cheese, grated
75g sun-dried tomatoes (drained if in oil), chopped
1 tablespoon crushed garlic
2 teaspoons chopped fresh or
   1 teaspoon dried oregano
1 tablespoon chopped fresh basil
2 eggs, lightly beaten
125ml milk
Salt and freshly ground black pepper, to taste
300g plain flour
1 tablespoon baking powder

1 Preheat the oven to 190°C/375°F/Gas mark 5. Grease a 12-cup muffin tin or line the cups with paper muffin cases.

2 Heat 1½ tablespoons of the olive oil in a large frying pan. Add the mushrooms and cook over a high heat for about 5 minutes, stirring frequently, until golden and tender. Remove the pan from the heat and set aside to cool.

3 Mix the pepperoni, ham, onion, mozzarella cheese, sun-dried tomatoes, garlic, oregano, basil and cooled mushrooms together in a bowl.

4 In a separate bowl or jug, mix the eggs, milk and remaining olive oil together, then add this to the pepperoni mixture. Season to taste with salt and pepper.

5 Mix the flour and baking powder together in a separate large bowl. Add the pepperoni mixture and mix briefly until just combined.

6 Spoon the batter into the prepared muffin cups, dividing it evenly. Bake in the oven for 20–25 minutes, or until risen and golden. Cool in the tin for 10 minutes, then turn out onto a wire rack. These muffins are best served warm.

Smoked Bacon
& Blue Cheese Muffins

Makes 12

225g rindless smoked streaky bacon
   rashers
300g plain flour
1 tablespoon baking powder
½ teaspoon salt
80g caster sugar
1 egg, lightly beaten
175ml milk
About 10 fresh basil leaves, finely
   chopped
75g blue cheese, crumbled
65g walnuts, chopped

1 Preheat the oven to 180°C/350°F/Gas mark 4. Grease a 12-cup muffin tin or line the cups with paper muffin cases.

2 Cook the bacon in a large frying pan (or under a preheated grill) until crisp. Remove the bacon from the pan and drain on kitchen paper. Set aside to cool. Reserve about 5 tablespoons of the bacon fat (or substitute vegetable oil). Break or chop the bacon into small pieces and set aside.

3 Mix the flour, baking powder, salt and sugar together in a large bowl. In a separate bowl or jug, mix the reserved bacon fat (or vegetable oil), egg, 5 tablespoons of water and milk together. Add the wet ingredients all at once to the dry ingredients, together with the bacon, basil, blue cheese and walnuts, and mix briefly until just combined.

4 Spoon the batter into the prepared muffin cups, dividing it evenly. Bake in the oven for 20–25 minutes, or until risen and golden. Cool in the tin for 10 minutes, then turn out onto a wire rack. Serve warm.

COOKIES

- Russian Teacakes
- Blueberry Thumbprint Cookies
- Oatmeal Raisin Cookies
- Polenta & Cranberry Cookies
- Malted Drop Cookies
- Butter Cookies
- Citrus Cream Clouds
- Lemon Macadamia Nut Cookies
- Fig & Date Rolls
- Traditional Choc Chip Cookies
- Fruity Oat Bites
- Nutty Jam Slices
- Teddies on a Stick
- Gypsy Creams

- Snickerdoodles
- Chocolate & Vanilla Whirls
- Refrigerator Sugar Cookies
- Ice Cream Sandwich Cookies
- Walnut Kisses
- Smilies
- Nutty Bubble Bars
- Melting Moments
- Easter Bonnets
- Peppermint Choc Sticks
- Toffee Apple Cookies
- Snowflake Cookies
- Blueberry Shortcake Cookies
- Chocolate Thumbprint Cookies

- Hazelnut & Chocolate Bars
- Lavender-Scented Shortbread
- Pineapple Macaroons
- Apricot & Almond Slices
- Hazelnut & Cinnamon Meringues
- Strawberry Jam Delights
- Mocha Mud Pies
- Blondies
- Savoury Whirls
- Oat Cakes
- Blue Cheese & Poppy Seed Cookies
- Cheesy Crumbles
- Sesame Cheese Twists

CHAPTER THREE

COOKIES

Russian Teacakes

Makes 20

115g unsalted butter, softened
2 teaspoons orange flower water
50g icing sugar
90g plain flour
25g lightly toasted ground walnuts
25g lightly toasted walnut pieces,
   chopped
Sifted icing sugar, for dusting

Tip
Always pay special
attention when measuring
flour – too much and your
cookies will be too hard;
too little and they will
turn out too flat.

1 Preheat the oven to 180°C/350°F/Gas mark 4. Line two or three baking sheets with non-stick baking paper. Beat the butter in a bowl until soft and creamy.

2 Beat in the orange flower water. Add the icing sugar and beat until fluffy. Add the flour and ground and chopped walnuts and mix well bringing the mixture together with your hands. Don't overwork the dough. Wrap the dough in clingfilm and chill in the refrigerator if the mixture is a little too soft.

3 Lightly dust your hands with flour and roll the mixture into balls or shape pieces of dough into logs about 7.5cm long. Curve each one into a crescent shape and place well apart on the prepared baking sheets.

4 Bake in the oven for about 15 minutes, or until firm and still pale in colour. Cool on the baking sheets for about 5 minutes, then dust liberally with sifted icing sugar. Transfer to a wire rack and leave to cool completely.

Blueberry Thumbprint Cookies

Makes 36

225g unsalted butter, softened
100g icing sugar
1 teaspoon vanilla extract
100g ground almonds
200g plain flour
Blueberry jam, for filling
Sifted icing sugar, for dusting

Tip

If you're cooking with children, make sure you clear a large work area – a small confined area may cause unnecessary accidents.

1 Lightly grease two baking sheets. Cream the butter and sugar together in a bowl until pale and fluffy, then beat in the vanilla extract. Mix in the ground almonds, then gradually add the flour, bringing the mixture together with your hands to form a soft dough as you add the last of the flour.

2 Lightly dust your hands with flour and roll the dough into small balls each about the size of a walnut. Arrange the dough balls on the prepared baking sheets, then, using your thumb, make a deep indent in the centre of each ball. Cover with cling film and chill in the refrigerator for 30 minutes.

3 Meanwhile, preheat the oven to 180°C/350°F/ Gas mark 4. Bake the cookies in the oven for 10 minutes, then remove from the oven and fill the indent in each cookie with a little jam. Return to the oven and bake for a further 5 minutes, or until pale golden.

4 Cool on the baking sheets for a few minutes, then transfer to a wire rack and leave to cool completely. Dust with sifted icing sugar to finish.

Oatmeal Raisin
Cookies

Makes 10–12

150g plain flour
150g rolled oats
1 teaspoon ground ginger
$\frac{1}{2}$ teaspoon baking powder
$\frac{1}{2}$ teaspoon bicarbonate of soda
150g soft light brown sugar
50g raisins
1 egg, lightly beaten
125ml vegetable oil
4 tablespoons milk

1 Preheat the oven to 200°C/400°F/Gas mark 6. Lightly grease a baking sheet. Mix the flour, oats, ginger, baking powder, bicarbonate of soda, sugar and raisins together in a large bowl.

2 In a separate bowl, mix the egg, vegetable oil and milk together. Make a well in the centre of the dry ingredients and pour in the egg mixture. Mix together well to make a soft dough.

3 Place spoonfuls of the dough well apart on the prepared baking sheet and flatten them slightly with the tines of a fork.

4 Bake in the oven for about 10 minutes, or until golden. Transfer to a wire rack to cool completely.

Polenta & Cranberry
Cookies

Makes 16

80g cold unsalted butter, cut
  into small pieces
100g fine polenta or cornmeal, plus
  extra for dusting
115g plain flour
50g caster sugar
1 egg, lightly beaten
Finely grated zest of 1 orange
100g dried sweetened cranberries

Tip
Only grease baking
sheets when a recipe
instructs you to, otherwise
the cookies may spread too
much and become flat.

1 Preheat the oven to 190°C/375°F/Gas mark 5.
Put the butter, polenta or cornmeal and flour in
a bowl. Rub in the butter until the mixture
resembles breadcrumbs, then stir in the sugar.

2 Add the egg, orange zest and cranberries and
mix together well with your hands until the
mixture just comes together.

3 Shape the mixture into small sticks and roll
each stick in extra polenta or cornmeal. Place
the sticks on two non-stick baking sheets, leaving a
little space between each one.

4 Bake in the oven for about 8–10 minutes, or
until just beginning to brown. Cool on the
baking sheets for 2–3 minutes, then transfer to a
wire rack and leave to cool completely.

Malted Drop Cookies

Makes 18

125g unsalted butter, softened
100g caster sugar
1 egg, lightly beaten
1 teaspoon vanilla extract
5 tablespoons malted
    chocolate powder
100g plain flour
50g rolled oats

Tip
To prevent baking paper slipping off baking sheets, sprinkle the baking sheet with a few drops of water beforehand.

1 Preheat the oven to 190°C/375°F/Gas mark 5. Line two baking sheets with non-stick baking paper.

2 Cream the butter and sugar together in a bowl until pale and fluffy. Beat in the egg and vanilla extract. Sift the malted chocolate powder and flour together, then beat them into the creamed mixture together with the oats until all the ingredients are well combined.

3 Drop heaped teaspoonfuls of the mixture onto the prepared baking sheets, spacing them well apart. Bake in the centre of the oven for 10–12 minutes, or until just golden. The lower baking sheet may need slightly longer.

4 Cool the cookies on the baking sheets for a few minutes, then transfer to a wire rack and leave to cool completely.

Butter Cookies

Makes 10–12

225g plain flour
1/2 teaspoon salt
1 teaspoon baking powder
Pinch of bicarbonate of soda
175g cold unsalted butter, cut into
    small pieces
6 tablespoons cold buttermilk
15g unsalted butter, melted, for
    brushing

1 Line a baking sheet with non-stick baking paper Sift the flour, salt, baking powder and bicarbonate of soda into a mixing bowl. Rub in the butter until the mixture resembles coarse breadcrumbs.

2 Stir in half the buttermilk and begin mixing the dough together, adding just enough of the remaining buttermilk to make a soft dough. Turn the dough onto a floured surface and dust with flour. Roll out the dough to form a rectangle about 2.5cm thick. Lift the dough from the surface and fold it into thirds. Give the dough a quarter turn. Flour the surface and dough again and re-roll into a rectangle of the same thickness. Repeat the folding and turning.

3 Transfer the dough to the prepared baking sheet. Cover with cling film and chill in the refrigerator for about 20 minutes.

4 Remove the dough from the refrigerator and repeat the rolling and folding twice more. Roll a final time to a rectangle about 2cm thick. Now either cut the dough into triangles or use a biscuit cutter to cut the dough into rounds.

5 Place the dough shapes about 2.5cm apart on the prepared baking sheet. Cover with cling film and chill in the refrigerator for at least 20 minutes.

6 Meanwhile, preheat the oven to 240°C/475°F/ Gas mark 9. Brush the tops of the cookies with melted butter and transfer to the oven. Reduce the oven temperature to 190°C/375°F/Gas mark 5. Bake for about 12–15 minutes, or until golden all over. Cool on the baking sheet for 5 minutes, then transfer to a wire rack and leave to cool completely. Serve warm or cold.

Citrus Cream Clouds

Makes 18

180g unsalted butter, softened
1 teaspoon finely grated lime zest
80g icing sugar
225g plain flour
40g cornflour

For the filling

125g unsalted butter, softened
1 teaspoon vanilla extract
1 teaspoon finely grated orange zest
1 teaspoon finely grated lemon zest
160g icing sugar, sifted, plus extra
   for dusting

Tip

Cool cookies on wire racks spaced apart without touching each other to keep them from sticking.

1 For the dough, beat the butter, lime zest and icing sugar together in a bowl until smooth and creamy. Stir in the flour and cornflour to make a dough, then knead until smooth. Wrap the dough in cling film and chill in the refrigerator for 30 minutes, or until firm.

2 Meanwhile, preheat the oven to 180°C/350°F/ Gas mark 4. Line two or three baking sheets with non-stick baking paper. Roll out half the dough between two sheets of non-stick baking paper. Using a flower-shaped biscuit cutter or a cutter of your choice, cut out eighteen 4cm shapes.

3 Add any trimmings of dough to the remaining pastry, roll out as before and cut out eighteen 6cm shapes. Place the dough shapes about 2.5cm apart on the prepared baking sheets.

4 Bake in the oven for about 5–6 minutes for the small shapes and 7–8 minutes for the large shapes, or until lightly browned. Transfer to a wire rack and leave to cool completely.

5 Put all the filling ingredients in a bowl and beat together until smooth and creamy. Either pipe or spread the filling onto each of the larger cookies. Top each one with a smaller cookie. Dust with sifted icing sugar to serve.

Lemon Macadamia Nut Cookies

Makes 24

125g unsalted butter, softened
100g caster sugar
2 egg yolks
Finely grated zest of ½ lemon
3 tablespoons freshly squeezed lemon
    juice
225g plain flour
6 tablespoons cornflour
100g macadamia nuts, lightly chopped

1 Preheat the oven to 190°C/375°F/Gas mark 5. Lightly grease two baking sheets.

2 Cream the butter and sugar together in a bowl until pale and fluffy. Beat in the egg yolks, lemon zest and lemon juice.

3 Sift the flour and cornflour into the mixture and beat until well combined. Add the macadamia nuts and stir until well mixed.

4 Drop heaped tablespoonfuls of the dough onto the prepared baking sheets, then flatten them slightly with the back of a spoon.

5 Bake in the oven for 10-12 minutes, or until golden. Cool on the baking sheets for a few minutes, then transfer to a wire rack and leave to cool completely.

Fig & Date Rolls

Makes 24

125g unsalted butter, softened
75g caster sugar
1 teaspoon ground cinnamon
1 egg, lightly beaten
75g ground almonds
225g plain flour

For the filling
300g dried figs, finely chopped
80g stoned dried dates, finely chopped
Finely grated zest of 1 lemon
100g caster sugar

1 For the filling, put all the ingredients together with 125ml of water in a saucepan and stir over a gentle heat until the sugar has dissolved. Simmer, uncovered, for about 15 minutes, or until the mixture is thick and pulpy. Remove the pan from the heat and set aside to cool.

2 For the dough, beat the butter, sugar, cinnamon and egg together in a bowl. Stir in the ground almonds and flour, mixing to make a dough. Knead the dough lightly, then divide it into four equal portions. Wrap each portion in cling film and chill in the refrigerator for 30 minutes.

3 Meanwhile, preheat the oven to 180°C/350°F/ Gas mark 4. Roll out each portion of dough between two sheets of non-stick baking paper to form a rectangle about 10 x 20cm in size.

4 Spread a quarter of the filling along each rectangle, leaving a 1cm border around the edges. Fold the long sides over the filling to meet in the centre and press gently together. Tuck the ends of each rectangle under.

5 Place the rolls, seam-side down, on non-stick baking sheets. Bake in the oven for 20–25 minutes, or until lightly browned. Transfer to a wire rack to cool. When cold, cut into slices. These cookies keep well in an airtight container for several days.

Traditional Choc Chip
Cookies

Makes 14

140g unsalted butter, softened
150g caster sugar
1 egg, lightly beaten
$\frac{1}{2}$ teaspoon vanilla extract
200g plain flour
1 teaspoon baking powder
150g plain chocolate chips
150g white chocolate chips

1 Preheat the oven to 180°C/350°F/Gas mark 4. Lightly grease two baking sheets.

2 Cream the butter and sugar together in a bowl until pale and fluffy. Beat in the egg and vanilla extract. Sift the flour and baking powder together, then beat these into the creamed mixture. Add all the chocolate chips and stir until well combined.

3 Drop 6-7 rounded tablespoonfuls of the dough onto each prepared baking sheet, spacing them well apart, as the cookies will almost double in size during baking.

4 Bake in the oven for 12–15 minutes, or until golden. Cool on the baking sheets for 2-3 minutes, then transfer to a wire rack and leave to cool completely. Store in an airtight container for up to five days.

Tip
Never drop cookies onto a hot baking sheet. Use two baking sheets if instructed to, or cool the sheet in between batches.

Fruity Oat Bites

Makes 10

150g unsalted butter cut
    into small pieces
75g soft light brown sugar
75g clear honey
175g muesli
75g rolled oats
100g ready-to-eat dried apricots,
    chopped
100g ready-to-eat dried apple
    rings, chopped
100g ready-to-eat dried
    mango, chopped

1 Preheat the oven to 190°C/375°F/Gas mark 5. Lightly grease a 20cm square cake tin and line the base with non-stick baking paper.

2 Melt the butter, sugar and honey together in a saucepan over a gentle heat, stirring until smooth and well combined.

3 Remove the pan from the heat and stir in the muesli, oats, apricots, apple and mango, mixing well. Press the mixture evenly into the prepared tin.

4 Bake in the oven for 20–25 minutes, or until lightly browned. Cool in the tin for a few minutes, then cut into 10 bars. Leave to cool completely in the tin before removing and serving. Store in an airtight container for up to two weeks.

Tip
Always bake cookies on the middle rack of your oven and preheat the oven to the required temperature at least 10 minutes before you are ready to cook.

Nutty Jam Slices

Makes 20

50g unsalted butter, softened
50g caster sugar
1 egg, separated
1 teaspoon almond extract
100g plain flour
25g ground almonds
25g flaked almonds
Jam of your choice, for filling

1 Lightly grease a baking sheet. Cream the butter and sugar together in a bowl until pale and fluffy. Beat in the egg yolk and almond extract. Work in the flour and ground almonds to form a firm dough, adding a little extra flour if the mixture is too soft.

2 Divide the dough in half and roll each portion of dough into a log about 25cm long. Place on the prepared baking sheet.

3 Lightly beat the egg white in a small bowl, then brush it over each log. Lightly crush the flaked almonds and press onto the logs, covering them completely. Flatten each log slightly.

4 Use the handle of a wooden spoon to press a channel down the centre of each log. Fill the hollows with jam. Cover with cling film and chill in the refrigerator for 30 minutes.

5 Meanwhile, preheat the oven to 180°C/350°F/ Gas mark 4. Bake the logs in the oven for 10–12 minutes, or until pale golden brown.

6 Leave the logs on the baking sheet until the jam has set but the dough is still warm. Cut each log diagonally into even slices, then transfer to a wire rack and leave to cool completely.

Teddies on a Stick

Makes 25

For the pale cookie dough
180g plain flour
$\frac{1}{2}$ teaspoon ground cinnamon
$\frac{1}{4}$ teaspoon bicarbonate of soda
50g cold unsalted butter, cut into small pieces
100g soft light brown sugar
2 tablespoons golden syrup
1 egg, beaten

For the dark cookie dough
180g plain flour
$\frac{1}{2}$ teaspoon ground ginger
$\frac{1}{4}$ teaspoon bicarbonate of soda
50g cold unsalted butter, cut into small pieces
100g soft dark brown sugar
2 tablespoons black treacle
1 egg, beaten

To serve
Wooden lolly sticks
Plain and white chocolate chips

1 Preheat the oven to 190°C/375°F/Gas mark 5. Line two or three baking sheets with non-stick baking paper. Make up the pale and dark cookie doughs in the same way, as follows.

2 Sift the flour, spice and bicarbonate of soda into a bowl. Rub in the butter until the mixture resembles fine breadcrumbs, then stir in the sugar. Set aside. Warm the syrup or treacle in a small saucepan over a gentle heat, then add this together with the eggs to the flour mixture. Mix and knead the ingredients together to form a smooth dough.

3 Roll out the dough on a lightly floured surface and, using a 6cm plain round biscuit cutter, stamp out rounds from the pale and dark doughs. Place the rounds on the prepared baking sheets. Insert a lolly stick into the base of each round.

4 Roll out the trimmings from each batch of dough and, using a 2.5cm plain round biscuit cutter, stamp out two rounds for each cookie. Place one small round on each cookie for the nose, using the pale dough for the dark faces and vice versa. Cut the other small round in half and place on the face for the ears. Mark the nose with a knife.

5 Bake in the oven for 8–10 minutes, or until lightly browned. Remove from the oven and, while still warm, position the chocolate chips for eyes. Transfer to a wire rack and leave to cool completely.

Gypsy Creams

Makes 10

50g unsalted butter, softened
50g white vegetable margarine
50g caster sugar
100g plain flour
50g rolled oats
1 tablespoon unsweetened cocoa
   powder

For the filling
50g unsalted butter, softened
75g icing sugar
2 tablespoons unsweetened
   cocoa powder

Tip
If you reduce the fat or
sugar content, cookies will
have a more cake-like
consistency

1 Preheat the oven to 180°C/350°F/Gas mark 4. Lightly grease a baking sheet.

2 For the cookie dough, cream the butter, margarine and sugar together in a bowl until pale and fluffy. Add all the remaining ingredients and beat together to form a dough.

3 Roll the dough into small balls and place on the prepared baking sheet. Flatten the dough balls with the tines of a fork dipped in hot water.

4 Bake in the oven for about 20 minutes, or until lightly browned. Remove from the oven and leave to cool completely on the baking sheet.

5 For the filling, beat the butter in a bowl until fluffy, then gradually beat in the icing sugar and cocoa powder until well mixed. Sandwich the cookies together in pairs with the filling.

Snickerdoodles

Makes 36

175g unsalted butter, softened
225g caster sugar
1 egg, lightly beaten
1 teaspoon vanilla extract
300g plain flour
1 teaspoon cream of tartar
½ teaspoon bicarbonate of soda

For the coating
1 tablespoon caster sugar
1 teaspoon ground cinnamon

Tip
You could also try
making wholemeal
snickerdoodles by substituting
115g of wholemeal flour
for 115g of the
plain flour.

1 Preheat the oven to 200°C/400°F/Gas mark 6. Lightly grease two baking sheets.

2 For the cookie dough, cream the butter and sugar together in a bowl until pale and fluffy. Beat in the egg and vanilla extract. Sift the flour, cream of tartar and bicarbonate of soda together into a separate bowl, then mix them into the butter mixture to form a soft dough.

3 Break off pieces of the dough about the size of a small walnut and roll into balls. For the coating, mix the sugar and cinnamon together in a bowl, then roll each dough ball in the cinnamon sugar, coating it all over.

4 Arrange the coated dough balls on the prepared baking sheets, spaced well apart. Bake in the oven for 8–10 minutes, or until pale golden. Transfer to a wire rack to cool.

Chocolate & Vanilla
Whirls

Makes 30

175g unsalted butter, softened
90g icing sugar
1 teaspoon vanilla extract
230g plain flour
2 tablespoons chocolate hazelnut
    spread, such as Nutella
1 tablespoon unsweetened
    cocoa powder

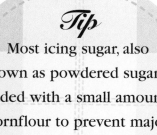

Tip
Most icing sugar, also
known as powdered sugar, is
blended with a small amount of
cornflour to prevent major
lumping. Even so, it's usually
best to sift it prior
to use.

1 Lightly grease two baking sheets. Cream the butter and sugar together in a bowl until pale and fluffy. Beat in the vanilla extract. Add the flour and mix to form a soft dough.

2 Divide the dough in half and work the chocolate hazelnut spread and cocoa powder evenly into one half.

3 Roll out each piece of dough on a lightly floured surface to form a 15 x 20cm rectangle. Place one rectangle of dough on top of the other and press together lightly. Trim the edges and roll up lengthways like a Swiss roll. Cover with cling film and chill in the refrigerator for 30 minutes.

4 Meanwhile, preheat the oven to 170°C/325°F/Gas mark 3. Cut the dough into 5mm slices and place them well apart on the prepared baking sheets.

5 Bake in the oven for 10-12 minutes, or until golden. Cool for 2-3 minutes on the baking sheets, then transfer to a wire rack and leave to cool completely.

Refrigerator Sugar Cookies

Makes 45

275g unsalted butter, softened
200g caster sugar
1 egg, lightly beaten
1 teaspoon vanilla extract
350g plain flour
Coloured sugar sprinkles,
    to decorate

Tip
Preheat the oven
for at least 10
minutes prior
to baking.

1 Cream the butter and sugar together in a bowl until pale and fluffy. Beat in the egg and vanilla extract. Stir in the flour, mixing to form a soft dough.

2 Shape the dough into a long log about 5cm in diameter. Spread the sugar sprinkles on a sheet of non-stick baking paper and roll the log in the sugar sprinkles until well coated all over.

3 Wrap the log in another sheet of non-stick baking paper and chill in the refrigerator until firm. At this point the dough can be stored in the refrigerator for up to one week, or placed in a plastic bag and frozen for up to two months.

4 When ready to bake, preheat the oven to 190°C/375°F/Gas mark 5. Lightly grease two baking sheets. Cut the log into slices 3mm thick and arrange the slices carefully on the prepared baking sheets, spaced well apart.

5 Bake in the oven for 8–10 minutes, or until just firm. Cool on the baking sheets for a few minutes, then transfer to a wire rack and leave to cool completely.

Ice Cream Sandwich
Cookies

Makes 10

115g unsalted butter, softened
115g caster sugar
1 egg, beaten
200g plain flour
25g unsweetened cocoa powder, sifted
100g plain chocolate chips
Chocolate or vanilla ice cream,
  softened

Tip
You can use any flavour
of ice cream for these
sweet treats: choc chip,
coconut, raspberry
ripple, praline, etc.

1 Preheat the oven to 180°C/350°F/Gas mark 4. Line one or two baking sheets with non-stick baking paper.

2 Cream the butter and sugar together in a bowl until pale and fluffy, then beat in the egg. Stir in the flour, cocoa powder and chocolate chips, mixing to form a firm dough.

3 Roll out the dough on a sheet of non-stick baking paper, then cut the dough into 20 rectangles each about 7.5 x 6cm in size. Place the dough rectangles on the prepared baking sheets. Bake in the oven for about 15 minutes or until firm. Transfer to a wire rack to cool completely.

4 Spread two good spoonfuls of softened ice cream on a cookie and press a second cookie on top. Squeeze so that the filling reaches the edges. Eat straightaway or wrap individually in foil and freeze. The filled cookies may be kept for up to two weeks in the freezer.

Walnut Kisses

Makes 40

50g walnuts
100g icing sugar
2 egg whites

Tip

Almonds work just as well as walnuts in this recipe.

1 Preheat the oven to 150ºC/300ºF/Gas mark 2. Line two baking sheets with non-stick baking paper. Process the walnuts in a food processor until they are very finely chopped. Sift the icing sugar into a bowl.

2 Put the egg whites in a separate large, grease-free, heat-proof bowl and whisk until frothy. Gradually add the sugar and whisk until combined.

3 Set the bowl over a pan of gently simmering water and, using a hand-held electric mixer, whisk until the mixture is very thick and stands in stiff peaks. Remove the bowl from the pan and whisk until cold.

4 Carefully fold in the ground walnuts until just blended, then spoon the mixture into a piping bag fitted with a large plain or star nozzle. Pipe small rosettes or balls onto the prepared baking sheets, spacing them slightly apart.

5 Bake in the oven for about 30 minutes, or until the cookies can be easily removed from the paper. Transfer to a wire rack to cool completely. Store in an airtight container.

Smilies

Makes 16

For the vanilla cookie dough
125g unsalted butter, softened
50g caster sugar
150g plain flour

For the chocolate cookie dough
125g unsalted butter, softened
50g caster sugar
130g plain flour
2 tablespoons unsweetened cocoa
    powder
2 tablespoons drinking chocolate
    powder

1 Preheat the oven to 180°C/350°F/Gas mark 4. Lightly grease one or two baking sheets. For each flavour of cookie dough, cream the butter and sugar together in a bowl until pale and fluffy. Gradually mix in the remaining ingredients to form a soft dough.

2 Roll out the vanilla cookie dough on a lightly floured surface to about 5mm thick. Using a 7.5cm plain round biscuit cutter, stamp out biscuit faces. Place on a prepared baking sheet. Reserve the dough trimmings.

3 Roll out the chocolate cookie dough in the same way. Cut out mouths, eyes, noses and hair, and gently place on the vanilla faces. Curve the mouths up for smilies – maybe one turned down for sad.

4 Cut out chocolate faces as before, place on a prepared baking sheet and use vanilla trimmings for the features as before.

5 Bake in the oven for about 10–12 minutes. Cool for a few minutes on the baking sheets, then transfer to a wire rack and leave to cool completely.

Nutty Bubble Bars

Makes 24

125g unsalted butter, cut into
    small pieces
5 tablespoons golden syrup
80g smooth peanut butter
100g caster sugar
70g plain puffed rice cereal, such as
    Rice Crispies
90g chocolate-flavoured puffed rice
    cereal, such as Coco Pops
50g peanut brittle, chopped
50g toasted hazelnuts, chopped

1 Grease a 24 x 30cm baking tin and line the base with non-stick baking paper. Mix the butter, golden syrup, peanut butter and sugar together in a medium saucepan. Heat gently, stirring, until the sugar has dissolved.

2 Bring the mixture to the boil, then reduce the heat and simmer very gently, uncovered and without stirring, for 5 minutes.

3 Remove the pan from the heat and stir in all the remaining ingredients, mixing well. Spoon the mixture into the prepared tin, spreading it evenly, then cover with cling film and chill in the refrigerator until set. Cut into bars to serve.

Tip

To prevent the golden syrup from clinging to the side of the measuring spoon, lightly grease the spoon first or spray it with non-stick cooking spray.

Melting Moments

Makes: 20

175g unsalted butter, softened
50g caster sugar
1 egg yolk
175g plain flour
Finely grated zest of ½ orange
    or lemon
1 tablespoon freshly squeezed orange
    or lemon juice
Mixed peel, to decorate
Sifted icing sugar, for dusting

Tip
Only store one kind of cookie in a container. If you mix crisp and soft cookies, they will all go soft and end up tasting the same.

1 Preheat the oven to 190°C/375°F/Gas mark 5. Lightly grease two baking sheets.

2 Cream the butter and sugar together in a bowl until pale and fluffy. Beat in the egg yolk, then work in the flour, orange or lemon zest and orange or lemon juice to form a smooth, thick paste.

3 Spoon the paste into a piping bag fitted with a large star nozzle and pipe rosettes of the mixture, each measuring about 5cm in diameter, onto the prepared baking sheets. Lightly press some mixed peel into the top of each cookie.

4 Bake in the oven for 15-20 minutes, or until pale golden. Cool on the baking sheets for a few minutes, then transfer to a wire rack and leave to cool completely. Dust each cookie with sifted icing sugar before serving.

Easter Bonnets

Makes 18

175g unsalted butter, softened
175g caster sugar
1 large egg, beaten
350g plain flour
1 teaspoon baking powder
1 teaspoon vanilla extract
Finely grated zest and juice of 1 small
   orange
500g ready-made white fondant icing
Edible coloured balls and ribbon, to
   decorate
Red and yellow food colouring
115g creamed coconut
50g icing sugar, plus extra for dusting

1 Cream the butter and caster sugar together in a bowl until pale and fluffy, then beat in the egg. Stir in the flour, baking powder, vanilla extract, orange zest and a little of the orange juice, mixing to form a soft, pliable dough. Wrap in cling film and chill in the refrigerator for 30 minutes.

2 Meanwhile, preheat the oven to 180°C/350°F/ Gas mark 4. Roll out the dough on a lightly floured surface to about 5mm thick and cut out 18 rounds with an 8cm plain round biscuit cutter.

3 Place the cookie rounds on two non-stick baking sheets, leaving a little space between each one. Bake in the oven for 10–12 minutes. Cool on the baking sheets for 10 minutes, then transfer to a wire rack and leave to cool completely.

4 Pinch off small balls of fondant icing and roll out on a surface dusted with icing sugar to about 3mm thick. Cut out tiny flower shapes to decorate the bonnets and push a coloured ball into the centre of each. Colour half of the remaining fondant icing pink and half yellow, then roll out each portion to about 3mm thick. Cut out nine 8cm rounds from each.

5 Warm the remaining orange juice in a small saucepan, then remove the pan from the heat and mix 2 tablespoons of the orange juice with the creamed coconut and icing sugar in a bowl to make a smooth paste.

6 Spoon a teaspoonful of the coconut paste onto the centre of each cookie. Cover with the rounds of coloured fondant and press down lightly to shape the bonnet. Decorate the bonnets with the ribbon and fondant flowers, securing them with a little icing sugar mixed with water. Leave to set before serving.

Peppermint Choc Sticks

Makes 12–15

250g plain chocolate, broken
   into squares
50g clear hard peppermints, crushed
150g amaretti biscuits, crushed

1 Melt the chocolate in a heat-proof bowl set over a pan of gently simmering water.

2 Remove the bowl from the heat and leave to cool slightly, then stir in the remaining ingredients, mixing well.

3 Place a 30 x 10cm sheet of non-stick baking paper on a baking sheet. Spread the chocolate mixture evenly over the paper, leaving a narrow border around the edge. Leave to set.

4 When firm, using a serrated-edged knife, carefully cut the chocolate mixture into relatively thin sticks to serve.

Tip
Because this is such an easy recipe to make, it gives you more time to be creative with the shape of the cookie. Instead of sticks, the mixture can be spread out and cut into thin squares or discs.

Toffee Apple Cookies

Makes 18

75g plain flour
½ teaspoon bicarbonate of soda
½ teaspoon ground cinnamon
150g unsalted butter, softened
180g soft light brown sugar
90g caster sugar
1 large egg, beaten
250g rolled oats
50g raisins
50g ready-to-eat dried apple rings,
    roughly chopped
50g chewy toffees, roughly chopped

1 Preheat the oven to 180°C/350°F/Gas mark 4. Line two or three baking sheets with non-stick baking paper. Sift the flour, bicarbonate of soda and cinnamon into a bowl and set aside.

2 Put the butter and both sugars in a separate bowl and beat together until creamy. Add the egg and beat well, then add the flour mixture and mix thoroughly. Add the oats, raisins and apple and toffee pieces and stir until just combined.

3 Using a small ice cream scoop or large tablespoon, place dollops of the cookie mixture onto the prepared baking sheets, spacing them well apart.

4 Bake in the oven for about 12–15 minutes, depending on size, or until lightly set in the centre and the edges are just beginning to brown.

5 Cool on the baking sheets for a few minutes and do not touch the cookies, as the melted toffee will be extremely hot and will set as the mixture cools down. Using a palette knife or spatula, transfer the slightly cooled cookies to a wire rack and leave to cool completely.

Snowflake Cookies

Makes 20

150g plain flour
115g cold unsalted butter, cut
   into small pieces
150g icing sugar
$\frac{1}{2}$ teaspoon ground cardamom
1 egg yolk
1 tablespoon milk
$\frac{1}{2}$ teaspoon vanilla extract
175g ready-made white fondant icing
1 tablespoon caster sugar
Edible small silver balls, to decorate

1 Put the flour, and half of the icing sugar in a bowl. Rub in the butter until the mixture resembles fine breadcrumbs. Add the cardamom, egg yolk, milk and vanilla extract and mix until it forms a soft dough. Gather the dough into a ball, wrap in cling film and chill in the refrigerator for 30 minutes.

2 Meanwhile, preheat the oven to 200°C/400°F/Gas mark 6. Roll out the dough on a lightly floured surface to 5mm thick and cut out 20 shapes using a snowflake paper template.

3 Place the dough shapes on two non-stick baking sheets, leaving a little space between each one. Bake in the oven for 6–8 minutes. Cool on the baking sheets for 10 minutes, then transfer to a wire rack and leave to cool completely.

4 Roll out the fondant icing on a surface lightly dusted with icing sugar to 3mm thick and cut out 20 snowflakes the same size as the cookies.

5 Mix the remaining icing sugar with 2 teaspoons of water in a bowl to make a smooth, thick glacé icing, then spoon the icing into a greaseproof paper piping bag and snip off the tip. Pipe small dots of icing over the cookies, then place the fondant icing snowflakes on top, pressing them down lightly to secure. Push the fondant icing in all around the shape to leave a small gap between the cookie and the fondant icing.

6 Use the remaining glacé icing to pipe snowflake lines over the fondant icing. Sprinkle immediately with the caster sugar and decorate with edible silver balls.

Berry Shortcake
Cookies

Makes 8

150g plain flour
1½ teaspoons baking powder
50g cold unsalted butter, cut into small
   pieces
50g granulated sugar
Finely grated zest of 1 lemon
125ml soured cream
100g fresh blueberries or strawberries
Crushed sugar lumps, for sprinkling

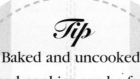

Tip
Baked and uncooked
shaped cookies can be frozen
for up to two months.
Thaw baked cookies at
room temperature and
bake uncooked ones
from frozen.

1 Preheat the oven to 190°C/375°F/Gas mark 5.
Line a baking sheet with non-stick baking paper.

2 Sift the flour and baking powder into a bowl.
Lightly rub in the butter until the mixture
resembles fine breadcrumbs. Stir in the granulated
sugar and lemon zest, then stir in the soured cream
and blueberries or strawberries, mixing until just
combined.

3 Spoon 8 mounds of the mixture onto the
prepared baking sheet, dividing it evenly and
placing the mounds well apart. Sprinkle with the
crushed sugar lumps.

4 Bake in the oven for about 20 minutes, or until
golden and firm in the centre. Transfer to a wire
rack to cool slightly. Serve warm and eat on the day
of baking.

Chocolate Thumbprint Cookies

Makes 24

50g plain chocolate, broken into
    squares
50g unsalted butter, softened
50g white vegetable margarine
50g caster sugar
175g plain flour

For the filling
75g plain, milk or white chocolate,
    broken into squares

1 For the cookie dough, melt the chocolate in a heat-proof bowl set over a pan of barely simmering water. Remove the bowl from the heat and set aside to cool.

2 Cream the butter, margarine and sugar together in a separate bowl until pale and fluffy. Beat in the melted chocolate, then add the flour and mix to form a smooth dough. Wrap in cling film and chill in the refrigerator for 30 minutes.

3 Meanwhile preheat the oven to 180°C/350°F/ Gas mark 4. Lightly grease one or two baking sheets. Shape the dough into 2.5cm balls and arrange them on the prepared baking sheets, spacing them well apart. Press your thumb into the centre of each ball to form an indent.

4 Bake in the oven for 10 minutes. Cool for a few minutes on the baking sheets, then transfer to a wire rack and leave to cool completely.

5 For the filling, melt the chocolate in a heat-proof bowl set over a pan of barely simmering water. Spoon the melted chocolate into the indent of each cookie and leave until set before serving.

Hazelnut & Chocolate
Bars

Makes 12

75g plain chocolate, broken
   into squares
125g unsalted butter, softened
50g soft light brown sugar
100g plain flour
75g rolled oats
12 tablespoons chocolate hazelnut
   spread, such as Nutella
50g hazelnuts, chopped and toasted

Tip
Keep the dough in the
freezer for those chocolate
cookie urges. Just remember to
thaw the dough in the
refrigerator for several hours
for easier slicing.

1 Preheat the oven to 180°C/350°F/Gas mark 4. Lightly grease a 20cm square cake tin and line the base with non-stick baking paper.

2 Melt the chocolate in a heat-proof bowl set over a pan of barely simmering water, stirring until smooth, then remove the bowl from the heat and set aside.

3 Cream the butter and sugar together in a separate bowl until pale and fluffy. Beat in the melted chocolate, then stir in the flour and oats, mixing to form a soft dough.

4 Press the mixture evenly into the base of the prepared tin. Bake in the oven for about 25 minutes, or until just golden. Remove from the oven and leave to cool completely in the tin.

5 Remove the baked mixture from the tin in one piece and spread the top evenly with the chocolate hazelnut spread. Sprinkle with the hazelnuts, pressing them lightly into the spread. Cut into bars. Store in a single layer in an airtight container, in a cool place, for up to one week.

Lavender-Scented
Shortbread

Makes 18–20

125g caster sugar
4 dried lavender flowers, natural and
   unsprayed
225g unsalted butter, softened
225g plain flour
120g ground rice
Pinch of salt
Extra caster sugar and dried lavender
   flowers, to decorate

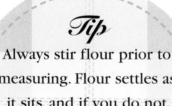

Tip
Always stir flour prior to
measuring. Flour settles as
it sits, and if you do not
stir it, you may end up
adding too much to
your cookies.

1 Line two baking sheets with greaseproof paper. Put the sugar and lavender flowers in a food processor and process for about 10 seconds.

2 Cream the butter and lavender sugar together in a bowl until pale and fluffy, then stir in the flour, ground rice and salt until the mixture resembles fine breadcrumbs.

3 Using your hands, gather the dough together and knead until it forms a ball. Roll the dough into a log, then shape it into a long, straight-edged block about 5cm in diameter. Wrap the dough in cling film and chill in the refrigerator for about 30 minutes, or until firm.

4 Meanwhile, preheat the oven to 190°C/375°F/ Gas mark 5. Slice the dough into 5mm squares and place on the prepared baking sheets.

5 Bake in the oven for 15–20 minutes, or until pale golden. Remove from the oven and sprinkle the cookies immediately with extra caster sugar. Leave to cool on the baking sheets for 10 minutes, then transfer to a wire rack and leave to cool completely. Decorate with extra lavender flowers before serving.

Pineapple Macaroons

Makes 20–24

400g can pineapple rings in natural
  juice
10–12 glacé cherries
3 egg whites
200g caster sugar
200g flaked or desiccated coconut

Tip

Vary the flavouring in
these chewy cookies or
leave out the pineapple if
you prefer a traditional
macaroon.

1 Preheat the oven to 170°C/325°F/Gas mark 3.
Line two or three baking sheets with non-stick
baking paper.

2 Drain the pineapple well and chop the fruit
finely. Place the chopped pineapple in a sieve
and squeeze out as much juice as possible. Halve
the glacé cherries and set aside.

3 Whisk the egg whites in a large bowl until
stiff peaks form. Gradually whisk in the sugar,
then fold in the pineapple and coconut until
well combined.

4 Drop spoonfuls of the mixture onto the
prepared baking sheets, piling the mixture into
pyramid shapes and leaving a little space between
each one, to allow the macaroons room to spread
slightly during baking. Top each one with a glacé
cherry half.

5 Bake in the oven for 25–30 minutes, or until
lightly browned and crisp. Remove from the
oven and leave the macaroons to cool completely
on the baking sheets, then carefully remove and
store them in an airtight container for up to three
days. Do not freeze.

Apricot & Almond Slices

Makes 16

300g plain flour
3 tablespoons icing sugar
1 teaspoon baking powder
175g cold unsalted butter, cut
    into small pieces
2 egg yolks

For the topping
60g apricot jam
2 egg whites
100g caster sugar
50g ground almonds
50g flaked almonds

For the glaze
60g apricot jam

1 Preheat the oven to 190°C/375°F/Gas mark 5. Lightly grease a 23cm square cake tin.

2 For the cookie dough, sift the flour, icing sugar and baking powder into a bowl. Rub in the butter until the mixture resembles fine breadcrumbs. Stir in the egg yolks.

3 Using your fingertips, work the mixture together to form a smooth dough, adding a little cold water if necessary. Roll or press out the dough to fit the base of the prepared tin, then prick it all over with a fork. Bake in the oven for about 10 minutes, or until just golden. Remove the tin from the oven.

4 To make the topping, spread the apricot jam over the part-baked crust in the tin. Whisk the egg whites in a bowl until frothy but not stiff. Stir in the sugar and ground almonds. Spread the almond mixture evenly over the jam, then sprinkle the flaked almonds over the top.

5 Return to the oven and bake for a further 20 minutes, or until golden brown. Remove from the oven and leave to cool in the tin. Once cold, carefully remove the pastry from the tin.

6 To make the glaze, melt the apricot jam with 1 tablespoon of water in a small saucepan, then brush this mixture evenly over the surface of the almond topping to glaze. Cut the glazed pastry into triangles or rectangles to serve.

Hazelnut & Cinnamon
Meringues

Makes 50

3 egg whites
150g caster sugar
85g ground hazelnuts
1 teaspoon ground cinnamon
250g milk chocolate, broken into
  squares

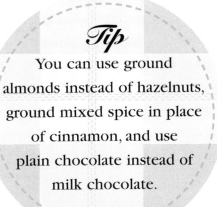

Tip
You can use ground
almonds instead of hazelnuts,
ground mixed spice in place
of cinnamon, and use
plain chocolate instead of
milk chocolate.

1 Preheat the oven to 120°C/250°F/Gas mark ½. Line three or four large baking sheets with non-stick baking paper.

2 Whisk the egg whites in a large bowl until the mixture soft peaks form. Whisk in the sugar a little at a time, whisking well between each addition. Fold in the ground hazelnuts and cinnamon.

3 Put the mixture into a piping bag fitted with a large plain nozzle. Pipe the mixture in 5cm rounds onto the prepared baking sheets. Flatten the tops with a wetted palette knife or spatula.

4 Bake in the oven for about 45 minutes, or until dry to the touch. Turn the oven off, leaving the meringues in the oven to dry out and cool.

5 Melt the chocolate in a heat-proof bowl set over a pan of barely simmering water, stirring until smooth. Either half-dip the meringues in the melted chocolate or just coat the edges of the meringues with chocolate. Leave to set on sheets of non-stick baking paper before serving.

Strawberry Jam
Delights

Makes 12–16

125g unsalted butter, softened
50g caster sugar
1 egg, lightly beaten
½ teaspoon vanilla extract
200g plain flour
6 tablespoons cornflour
½ teaspoon baking powder
Strawberry or raspberry jam,
   for filling

Tip

To vary this recipe, use a
mixed fruit jam, such as
peach and pear or blackberry
and apple, or even a speciality
marmalade, such as orange
or pineapple

1 Preheat the oven to 180°C/350°F/Gas mark 4. Lightly grease two baking sheets.

2 Cream the butter and sugar together in a bowl until pale and fluffy. Beat in the egg and vanilla extract. Sift the flour, cornflour and baking powder into the creamed mixture and beat together to form a soft dough.

3 Roll out the dough on a lightly floured surface to about 3mm thick, then cut into rounds using a 6cm plain biscuit cutter. Cut a 2.5cm circle from the centre of half of the rounds. Re-roll the trimmings to make additional cookies. Make sure you have an equal number of rounds and rings, then arrange them on the prepared baking sheets.

4 Bake in the oven for about 15 minutes, or until pale golden. Cool on the baking sheets for a few minutes, then transfer to a wire rack and leave to cool completely.

5 Spread the cookie rounds with some jam, then place a cookie ring on top of each round, pushing them lightly together. Store in an airtight container for up to one week.

Mocha Mud Pies

Makes 16

30g plain flour

¼ teaspoon bicarbonate of soda

200g plain chocolate, roughly chopped

25g unsalted butter, cut into small pieces

2–3 tablespoons instant coffee granules, to taste

2 large eggs

115g caster sugar

1 teaspoon vanilla extract

50g plain chocolate chips

1 Sift the flour and bicarbonate of soda into a bowl. Set aside. Melt the chocolate and butter together in a heat-proof bowl set over a pan of barely simmering water stirring until smooth. Remove the bowl from the heat and stir in the coffee granules. Set aside.

2 Put the eggs and sugar in a separate bowl and using a hand-held electric mixer, whisk until the mixture is pale and very thick. Stir in the melted chocolate mixture and vanilla extract until well combined. Stir in the flour mixture, then add the chocolate chips, mixing well. Cover the bowl and chill in the refrigerator for about 1 hour.

3 Meanwhile, preheat the oven to 180°C/350°F/Gas mark 4. Line two or three baking sheets with non-stick baking paper. Place spoonfuls of the cookie dough well apart on the prepared baking sheets.

4 Bake in the oven for about 10 minutes, or until the cookies feel just set when touched lightly with a finger. Cool on the baking sheets for a few minutes, then transfer to a wire rack and leave to cool completely.

Blondies

Makes 18

500g white chocolate, broken into
  squares
75g unsalted butter, cut into
  small pieces
3 eggs, lightly beaten
180g caster sugar
180g self-raising flour
180g macadamia nuts, roughly
  chopped
1 teaspoon vanilla extract

Tip
Store bar cookies either
in tightly covered containers
or in the tin in which they
were baked. Make sure you
cover the tin tightly
with foil.

1 Preheat the oven to 190°C/375°F/Gas mark 5. Grease a 26 x 19cm cake tin and line the base with non-stick baking paper.

2 Roughly chop 400g of the chocolate and set aside. Melt the remaining chocolate and the butter together in a heat-proof bowl set over a pan of barely simmering water, stirring until smooth. Remove the bowl from the heat and leave to cool slightly.

3 Beat the eggs and sugar together in a separate bowl, then gradually beat in the melted chocolate mixture. Sift the flour over the mixture and fold in together with the macadamia nuts, reserved chopped chocolate and the vanilla extract, mixing well.

4 Transfer the mixture to the prepared tin and level the surface. Bake in the oven for 30–35 minutes, or until the centre is only just firm to the touch. Remove from the oven and leave to cool completely in the tin. Cut into squares to serve.

Savoury Whirls

Makes 15

125g unsalted butter, softened
1 clove garlic, crushed
2 tablespoons soured cream
150g plain flour
$\frac{1}{2}$ teaspoon paprika
Salt and freshly ground black pepper,
    to taste

1 Preheat the oven to 190°C/375°F/Gas mark 5. Lightly grease two baking sheets.

2 Beat the butter in a bowl until creamy, then beat in the garlic, soured cream, flour, paprika and salt and pepper. Mix well to form a smooth paste.

3 Spoon the mixture into a piping bag fitted with a large star nozzle and pipe rosettes of the mixture onto the prepared baking sheets.

4 Bake in the oven for 12–15 minutes, or until golden. Cool on the baking sheets for a few minutes, then transfer to a wire rack and leave to cool completely.

Tip
Always measure ingredients accurately. Use glass measuring jugs for liquid ingredients, as it is more accurate to see the level of liquid.

Oat Cakes

Makes 12

100g rolled oats
50g plain flour
1 teaspoon bicarbonate of soda
1 teaspoon caster sugar
Pinch of salt
50g unsalted butter, cut into
    small pieces

Tip
Dip cutters in flour as
you go along to keep the
dough from sticking to them
and tearing the cookies.
Re-roll as little
as possible.

1 Preheat the oven to 180°C/350°F/Gas mark 4. Lightly grease a baking sheet.

2 Put the oats, flour, bicarbonate of soda, sugar and salt in a bowl and set aside. Put the butter and 1-2 tablespoons of water in a small saucepan and heat gently until the butter melts. Stir the melted butter mixture into the oat mixture and combine to form a dough.

3 Turn out the dough onto a lightly floured surface and knead until it is no longer sticky, adding a little extra flour if necessary.

4 Roll out the dough until it is about 7.5mm thick, then cut out rounds using a 7.5cm biscuit cutter. Arrange the rounds on the prepared baking sheet, then bake in the oven for 15-20 minutes, or until golden.

5 Transfer to a wire rack and leave to cool completely. Store in an airtight container for up to two weeks.

Blue Cheese
& Poppy Seed Cookies

Makes 25–30

150g plain flour
100g unsalted butter, softened
75g mild full-fat soft blue cheese
2 tablespoons poppy seeds

Tip

Always chill cookie dough in the refrigerator when instructed to do so. This will make the dough easier to work with when you are cutting it into slices ready to bake.

1 Put the flour, butter and blue cheese in a bowl and mix together until well combined. Place the mixture on a sheet of cling film and shape into a log about 4cm in diameter. Wrap in the cling film and chill in the refrigerator for about 1 hour until firm.

2 Meanwhile, preheat the oven to 180°C/350°F/ Gas mark 4. Unwrap the chilled dough, spread the poppy seeds on a sheet of non-stick baking paper and roll the cylinder of dough in the poppy seeds, coating it all over.

3 Cut the dough into even slices and place them about 3cm apart on one or two non-stick baking sheets.

4 Bake in the oven for about 10 minutes, or until lightly browned. Transfer to a wire rack and leave to cool completely.

Cheesy Crumbles

Makes 20

115g Cheddar cheese
4 spring onions
25g walnuts
100g plain flour
1 teaspoon wholegrain mustard
75g unsalted butter

1 Preheat the oven to 190°C/375°F/Gas mark 5. Lightly grease two baking sheets. Coarsely grate the cheese into a bowl. Thinly slice the spring onions and finely chop the walnuts, then stir them into the cheese. Stir in the flour and mustard.

2 Melt the butter in a saucepan over a gentle heat, then remove the pan from the heat and add the melted butter to the cheese mixture, stirring until well combined. Shape the mixture into 2.5cm balls and place on the prepared baking sheets. Flatten each one slightly with a palette knife or spatula.

3 Bake in the oven for about 15 minutes, or until golden brown. Leave to cool on the baking sheets for 2-3 minutes, then transfer to a wire rack and leave to cool completely.

Tip

These cookies are best eaten warm or on the day they are made, but they can be stored in an airtight container in a cool place for up to three days.

Sesame Cheese Twists

Makes 14

100g Cheddar cheese
125g unsalted butter, softened
200g plain flour
Beaten egg, to glaze
2 tablespoons sesame seeds

1 Preheat the oven to 200°C/400°F/Gas mark 6. Lightly grease two baking sheets. Finely grate the cheese, using the fine grater attachment of a food processor.

2 Remove the grating disc and insert the metal mixing blade. Place the butter in the food processor with the cheese and process until pale and creamy. Add the flour and process until the mixture comes together to form a ball of dough.

3 Roll out the dough on a lightly floured surface to about 3mm thick. Cut into strips each about 15cm long and 5cm wide. Take two strips at a time and twist them together. Pinch the ends together.

4 Arrange the twists on the prepared baking sheets. Brush with beaten egg and sprinkle with the sesame seeds.

5 Bake in the oven for 10–12 minutes, or until pale golden. Cool for a few minutes on the baking sheets, then transfer to a wire rack and leave to cool completely. Store in an airtight container for up to one week.

CUPCAKES

- Tarte Tatin Cupcakes
- Jam-Filled Cupcakes
- Apple Pie Cupcakes
- Chocolate Cupcake Pies
- Cherry Almond Pie Cupcakes
- Cookies 'n' Cream Cupcakes
- Blueberry Cream Cupcakes
- Chocolate Coconut Cupcakes
- Poppy Seed & Honey Cupcakes
- Strudel Cups
- Gingerbread Cupcakes
- Persimmon Nut Treats
- Strawberry Rhubarb Crisp Cupcakes
- S'mores Cupcakes

- Birthday Beauties
- Lemon Meringue Cupcakes
- Hot Chocolate & Marshmallow Cupcakes
- Brownie Cupcakes
- Rum Raisin Cupcakes
- Boston Cream Cupcakes
- Bourdaloue Cupcakes with Caramelized Almonds
- Chocolate Charlotte Cupcakes
- Cevenol Cupcakes
- Mendicant Cupcakes
- Opera Cupcakes
- Far Breton Cupcakes
- Irish Coffee Cupcakes
- Clafoutis with Crème Anglaise

- Frozen Lemon Cupcakes
- Mother's Day Rose Cupcakes
- July 4th Blueberry & Raspberry Cupcakes
- Easter Lavender Cupcakes
- Apple Cider Cupcakes
- Halloween Orange Cupcakes
- Mezzo-Mezzo Cupcakes
- Christmas Fruit Cupcakes
- New Year's Eve Confetti Cupcakes
- Pastis Cupcakes
- Kir Cupcakes
- After-Eight Cupcakes

CHAPTER FOUR

CUPCAKES

Tarte Tatin Cupcakes

Makes 16

250g plain flour
2 teaspoons baking powder
1 teaspoon salt
100g soft light brown sugar
125g unsalted butter, softened
2 eggs, lightly beaten
250ml milk
1 teaspoon vanilla extract

For the caramelized apples
65g unsalted butter, cut into small
   pieces
4 eating apples, peeled, cored and cut
   into 16 (cut each quarter into four
   equal pieces, lengthways)
4 tablespoons caster sugar

For the caramel glaze
65g unsalted butter
50g soft light brown sugar
225g icing sugar
1 teaspoon vanilla extract
1 tablespoon milk

1 Preheat the oven to 180°C/350°F/Gas mark 4. Grease 16 cups of two 12-cup tins or line 16 cups with paper cupcake cases.

2 For the cupcakes, mix the flour, baking powder, salt and sugar together in a bowl. Add all the remaining cupcake ingredients and beat together with a wooden spoon until thoroughly mixed.

3 Spoon the batter into the prepared cupcake cups, filling each one about two-thirds full. Bake in the oven for about 20 minutes, or until a skewer inserted into the centre comes out clean. Turn out onto a wire rack and leave to cool.

4 For the caramelized apples, melt the butter in a large saucepan, add the pieces of apple, and turn to cook them on both sides. When they are golden, sprinkle with the sugar, then remove the pan from the heat. Arrange them attractively on top of the cupcakes, four apple sections per cupcake. You may want to cook the apples in two batches.

5 To make the glaze, melt the butter in a heavy-based saucepan over a low heat. Add the brown sugar and stir until the sugar has melted.

6 Remove the pan from the heat. Add the icing sugar, vanilla extract and milk to the pan and beat together until smooth and well mixed. Drizzle about a tablespoon of the glaze over each cupcake before serving.

Jam-Filled Cupcakes

Makes 12

225g plain flour
2 teaspoons baking powder
1 teaspoon salt
125g unsalted butter, softened
200g caster sugar
2 eggs, lightly beaten
1 teaspoon vanilla extract (or another
flavouring, such as almond extract,
orange flower water, etc.)
250ml milk
Jam, marmalade or preserves of your
choice

For the icing
3 tablespoons hot milk or double cream
375g icing sugar

To decorate
Coloured sugars, sweets and stencils

1 Preheat the oven to 180°C/350°F/Gas mark 4.
Grease a 12-cup tin or line the cups with paper
cupcake cases. For the cupcakes, sift the flour,
baking powder and salt into a bowl and set aside.

2 Cream the butter and sugar together in a
separate bowl until pale and fluffy. Gradually add
the eggs, beating well after each addition. Add the
vanilla extract or other flavouring. Alternately add
the flour mixture and milk to the creamed mixture
and beat until the batter is smooth.

3 Spoon the batter into the prepared cupcake
cups, filling each cup about two-thirds full. Bake
in the oven for 20–25 minutes, or until a skewer
inserted into the centre comes out clean. Turn out
onto a wire rack and leave to cool completely.

4 Using a sharp knife, remove a cone from the
centre cup of each cupcake. Drop a teaspoon of
jam, marmalade or preserves of your choice into
each well and replace the scooped-out cones.

5 For the icing, put the hot milk or cream in a
large bowl. Gradually stir in the sugar until the
icing is thick enough to spread. Beat for several
minutes until the icing is smooth and creamy. You
may need to add more sugar or liquid to get the
right consistency, but remember to beat well after
each addition.

6 Spread some icing over the top of each cupcake.
While still soft, decorate with coloured sugars,
sweets, or stencils. Leave to set before serving.

Apple Pie Cupcakes

Makes 8 regular or 4 jumbo cupcakes

For the pastry cases

Enough pastry (shortcrust, puff, flaky, etc), either homemade or ready-made, to make two 23cm pies

For the filling

4–5 eating apples, peeled, cored and cut into pieces

1 tablespoon lemon juice

100g caster sugar, plus 2 tablespoons for sprinkling

Pinch of salt

Pinch of freshly grated nutmeg

1 teaspoon ground cinnamon

2 tablespoons plain flour

65g unsalted butter, softened

1 Preheat the oven to 230°C/450°F/Gas mark 8. Grease 8 cups of a 12-cup tin or regular silicone cupcake mould, or grease 4 cups of a 6 or 12-cup muffin tin or jumbo silicone cupcake mould, or line 8 or 4 cups with paper cupcake or muffin cases.

2 See Chocolate Cupcake Pies (page 205) for instructions on rolling out the pastry and lining the prepared tin or moulds. Reserve enough of the pastry dough to cut out rounds to cover the cupcakes.

3 For the filling, in a large bowl, toss the apples with the lemon juice, the 100g of sugar, the salt, nutmeg, cinnamon and flour, coating evenly. Scoop the mixture into the pastry cases and dot with the butter. Cover each cupcake with a round of dough, crimping the edges together for a pretty effect. Cut two vents in the top of each cupcake so that the steam can escape, then sprinkle the cupcakes with the remaining sugar.

4 Bake in the oven for 10 minutes, then reduce the oven temperature to 180°C/350°F/Gas mark 4. Bake for a further 15–20 minutes, or until the pastry is golden brown. Remove from the oven and leave the cupcakes to cool completely before removing them from the tin or mould.

Chocolate Cupcake Pies

Makes 14–16

For the pastry cases

Enough pastry (shortcrust, puff, flaky, etc), either homemade or ready-made, to make two 23cm pies

For the filling

125g plain chocolate, broken into squares
450ml double cream
130g caster sugar
5 eggs, lightly beaten

Walnut halves and/or whipped cream, to decorate (optional)

1 Preheat the oven to 180°C/350°F/Gas mark 4. Grease 14–16 cups of two 12-cup tins or regular silicone cupcake moulds, or line 14–16 cups with paper cupcake cases.

2 For the pastry cases, roll out the pastry on a lightly floured surface and cut out rounds each measuring 10cm in diameter. Line the prepared cupcake cups with the pastry rounds, folding the edge of the dough back under so that it will look pretty. Gently prick a few holes in the bottom of the pastry cups using a fork so that they don't buckle when cooked. Set aside.

3 For the filling, melt the chocolate in a large heat-proof bowl set over a pan of barely simmering water. Remove the bowl from the heat as soon as the chocolate has melted. Add the cream, sugar and eggs and beat until the ingredients are well combined.

4 Carefully pour the chocolate mixture into the prepared pastry cases, filling each case about three-quarters full. Bake in the oven for about 25 minutes, or until the chocolate filling is cooked. The filling will rise while cooking, but will fall when it cools. Remove from the oven and leave the cupcakes to cool completely before removing them from the tins or moulds.

5 Decorate each cupcake with a walnut half or a dollop of whipped cream, or both, if you like. If you are making the cupcakes in the silicone moulds or greased tins, turn out and serve them in pretty paper cupcake cases.

Cherry Almond Pie
Cupcakes

Makes 14–16

For the pastry cases
Enough pastry (shortcrust, puff, flaky, etc), either homemade or ready-made, to make two 23cm pies

For the filling
125g unsalted butter, softened
100g caster sugar
2 large eggs, lightly beaten
100g ground almonds
Finely grated zest of 1 lemon
325g stoned morello cherries (tinned cherries work wonderfully well, but you can use fresh or frozen depending on the season)

Sifted icing sugar, for dusting
Flaked almonds, to decorate

1 Preheat the oven to 180°C/350°F/Gas mark 4. Grease 14–16 cups of two 12-cup tins or regular silicone cupcake moulds, or line 14–16 cups with paper cupcake cases. See Chocolate Cupcake Pies (page 205) for instructions on rolling out the pastry and lining the prepared tins or moulds.

2 For the filling, cream the butter and sugar together in a bowl until pale and fluffy. Gradually add the eggs, beating well after each addition. Add the ground almonds and lemon zest and mix well.

3 Spoon the mixture into the prepared pastry cases, filling each case about half full. Press the cherries into the mixture, pushing them under the almond paste with your fingers.

4 Bake in the oven for 25–30 minutes, or until golden brown, puffed up and springy to the touch. Turn off the oven and leave the cupcakes in the oven with the door ajar for about 10 minutes.

5 Remove from the oven and leave the cupcakes to cool completely before removing them from the tins or moulds. Dust with sifted icing sugar and decorate with flaked almonds before serving.

Cookies 'n' Cream Cupcakes

Makes 18–20

250g plain flour
2 teaspoons baking powder
1 teaspoon salt
125g unsalted butter, cut into pieces
200g caster sugar
2 eggs, lightly beaten
1 teaspoon vanilla extract
175ml single cream
115g sandwich cookies or biscuits,
   coarsely crushed

For the icing
180g white chocolate, broken into
   squares
180g cream cheese or full-fat soft
   cheese, softened and cut into pieces
185g unsalted butter, cut into pieces

Miniature sandwich cookies or crushed
   cookies or biscuits, to decorate

1 Preheat the oven to 180°C/350°F/Gas mark 4. Grease 18–20 cups of two 12-cup tins or line 18–20 cups with paper cupcake cases. For the cupcakes, sift the flour, baking powder and salt into a bowl and set aside.

2 Cream the butter and sugar together in a separate bowl until light and fluffy. Gradually add the eggs, beating well after each addition. Add the vanilla extract. Alternately add the flour mixture and cream to the creamed mixture and beat until smooth. Fold in the crushed cookies or biscuits.

3 Spoon the batter into the prepared cupcake cups, filling each cup about two-thirds full. Bake in the oven for 20–25 minutes, or until a skewer inserted into the centre comes out clean. Turn out onto a wire rack and leave to cool.

4 To make the icing, melt the white chocolate in a large heat-proof bowl set over a pan of barely simmering water. It should be just warm to the touch. Remove the bowl from the heat.

5 Beat the cream cheese or soft cheese and butter together in a separate bowl until pale and fluffy. Add the melted chocolate and beat again until smooth. Use the icing immediately or it will harden. Spread some icing over the top of each cupcake, then top with a miniature cookie or sprinkle with crushed cookies or biscuits immediately, while the icing is still soft. Leave to set before serving.

Blueberry Cream Cupcakes

Makes 18

375g plain flour
3 teaspoons baking powder
1 teaspoon salt
125g unsalted butter, cut into small
  pieces
200g caster sugar
2 eggs, lightly beaten
250ml milk or single cream
225g fresh or frozen blueberries
  (thawed if frozen)

For the topping
250ml whipping cream
50g icing sugar, sifted
Dried blueberries, to decorate
  (optional)

1 Preheat the oven to 180°C/350°F/Gas mark 4.
Grease 18 cups of two 12-cup tins or regular
silicone cupcake moulds, or line 18 cups with
paper cupcake or muffin cases.

2 For the cupcakes, sift the flour, baking powder
and salt into a bowl and set aside. Cream the
butter and sugar together in a separate large bowl
until pale and fluffy. Gradually add the eggs, beating
well after each addition. Alternately add the flour
mixture and milk or cream to the creamed mixture,
mixing well.

3 Using a fork, crush 135g of the blueberries with
1 tablespoon of water in a small bowl until
soft. Save 45g for the topping. Add 90g to the batter
and mix thoroughly. Gently fold in the remaining
90g of whole blueberries.

4 Spoon the batter into the prepared cupcake
cups, filling each cup about two-thirds full.
Bake in the oven for 20–25 minutes, or until a
skewer inserted into the centre comes out clean.
Turn out onto a wire rack and leave to cool
completely.

5 For the topping, whip the cream in a bowl
until it starts to form soft peaks. Gradually add
the sugar, whisking continuously. Add the reserved
crushed blueberries and mix well.

6 Spoon or pipe onto the cupcakes and top with
a dried blueberry just before serving. Because
of their beautiful colour, you can leave them un-iced
and dust with sifted icing sugar if preferred.

Chocolate Coconut Cupcakes

Makes 12–14

250g plain flour
2 teaspoons baking powder
1 teaspoon salt, plus a pinch for the
   egg whites
3 eggs, separated
100g soft light brown sugar
125ml vegetable oil, plus 2 tablespoons
100g desiccated coconut, plus
   2 tablespoons for sprinkling
2 tablespoons unsweetened cocoa
   powder, plus extra for dusting
125g plain chocolate, grated
4 tablespoons milk
Chocolate pudding (instant, ready-
   made or homemade), for filling
Whipped cream, to decorate

1 Preheat the oven to 180°C/350°F/Gas mark 4. Grease 12–14 cups of one or two 12-cup tins or line 12–14 cups with paper cupcake cases. Sift the flour, baking powder and salt into a bowl and set aside.

2 With a whisk or a wooden spoon, mix the egg yolks and sugar together in a separate bowl. Add 125ml of vegetable oil and then the flour mixture, beating until the batter is smooth. Stir in the 100g of coconut, the cocoa powder, grated chocolate and milk, mixing well. Set aside.

3 Whisk the egg whites with a pinch of salt in a separate bowl until stiff but not dry. Gently fold the whisked egg whites into the chocolate batter.

4 Spoon the batter into the prepared cupcake cups, filling each cup about two-thirds full. Smooth the tops with the back of a spoon. Sprinkle a little coconut over each cupcake.

5 Bake in the oven for 10 minutes, then reduce the oven temperature to 150°C/300°F/Gas mark 2 and bake for a further 20 minutes, or until a skewer inserted into the centre comes out clean. Turn out onto a wire rack and leave to cool.

6 When the cupcakes are completely cool, using a sharp knife remove a cone from the centre of each cupcake and spoon some chocolate pudding into each well. Add a little dollop of whipped cream to decorate. Dust with sifted cocoa powder.

Poppy Seed & Honey
Cupcakes

Makes 24 regular or 12 jumbo cupcakes

200g poppy seeds
125ml clear honey
375g plain flour
1 teaspoon bicarbonate of soda
1 teaspoon salt, plus a good pinch for the egg whites
240g unsalted butter, softened
300g caster sugar
4 eggs, separated
1 teaspoon vanilla extract
250ml soured cream
Sifted icing sugar, for dusting

1 Preheat the oven to 180°C/350°F/Gas mark 4. Grease the cups of two 12-cup tins or regular silicone cupcake moulds, or grease the cups of a 12-cup muffin tin or jumbo silicone cupcake mould, or line 24 or 12 cups with paper cupcake or muffin cases.

2 Cook the poppy seeds with the honey and 4 tablespoons of water in a saucepan for about 5 minutes. Remove the pan from the heat and leave to cool. Sift the flour, bicarbonate of soda and salt into a bowl and set aside.

3 Cream the butter and caster sugar together in a separate large bowl until pale and fluffy. Add the cooled poppy seed mixture and mix well. Add the egg yolks, one at a time, beating well after each addition. Beat in the vanilla extract and soured cream. Add the flour mixture to the creamed mixture, stirring to mix well. Set aside.

4 In a separate bowl, whisk the egg whites with a good pinch of salt until stiff but not dry. Gently fold the whisked egg whites into the poppy seed batter. Spoon the batter into the prepared cupcake cups, filling each cup just a little over half full.

5 Bake in the oven for about 15 minutes, or until golden brown on top – the cooking time will depend on the size of the cupcakes you are making. Loosely cover the cupcakes with a piece of foil and bake for a further 5–10 minutes, or until a skewer inserted into the centre comes out clean. Turn out onto a wire rack and leave to cool. Dust with sifted icing sugar before serving.

Strudel Cups

Makes 12

For the pastry cases
225g filo pastry sheets
125g unsalted butter, melted

For the filling
4 medium cooking apples, peeled,
    cored and chopped
2 tablespoons lemon juice
100g caster sugar, or to taste
60g walnuts, chopped
25g raisins
1 teaspoon ground cinnamon
25g toasted breadcrumbs

Whipped cream, to serve (optional)

Tip
The purpose of the breadcrumbs in the filling is to absorb the excess liquid. You can use ground almonds instead for added flavour.

1 Preheat the oven to 180°C/350°F/Gas mark 4. Grease a 12-cup tin or regular silicone cupcake mould.

2 Cut the filo pastry sheets into 12cm squares. Put a square into each cup or mould. Brush with a little of the melted butter. Repeat five more times for each cupcake, staggering the corners of the square so that the sides of the cups or moulds are entirely covered. Flatten the dough with the pastry brush as you go.

3 To make the filling, put the apple pieces in a large bowl. Add the lemon juice and toss to coat the apples well so that they don't turn brown. Add all the remaining filling ingredients and mix well.

4 Put a heaped tablespoon of the filling in the centre of each cupcake. Using scissors or a very sharp knife, trim off any excess dough around the edges of the cups or moulds, or leave as is.

5 Bake for about 15–20 minutes, until the mixture is brown on top and the pastry is cooked. Remove from the oven and leave to cool. Turn out carefully and serve the cups individually on a plate, with a dollop of whipped cream, if you like.

Gingerbread Cupcakes

Makes 12

225g plain flour
2 teaspoons baking powder
1 teaspoon salt
1 teaspoon ground ginger
$\frac{1}{2}$ teaspoon ground cinnamon
$\frac{1}{2}$ teaspoon ground allspice
Pinch each of freshly grated nutmeg
   and ground cloves
125g unsalted butter, softened
150g soft light brown sugar
2 eggs, lightly beaten
1 teaspoon vanilla extract
1 heaped tablespoon finely grated
   (peeled) fresh root ginger
125ml milk
3 tablespoons finely chopped
   crystallized ginger

For the icing
125ml whipping cream, chilled
4 tablespoons icing sugar, sifted
$\frac{1}{2}$ teaspoon ground ginger, plus extra
   for dusting
1 teaspoon finely grated (peeled) fresh
   root ginger
Sliced crystallized ginger, to decorate

1 Preheat the oven to 180°C/350°F/Gas mark 4. Grease a 12-cup tin or line the cups with paper cupcake cases. For the cupcakes, sift the flour, baking powder, salt and spices into a bowl and set aside.

2 Cream the butter and sugar together in a separate large bowl until pale and fluffy. Gradually add the eggs, beating well after each addition. Add the vanilla extract and grated fresh ginger. Alternately add the flour mixture and milk to the creamed mixture, beating well until smooth. Fold in the crystallized ginger.

3 Spoon the batter into the prepared cupcake cups, filling each cup about two-thirds full. Bake in the oven for 20–25 minutes, or until a skewer inserted into the centre comes out clean. Turn out onto a wire rack and leave to cool.

4 To make the icing, whip the cream in a bowl until almost stiff. Gradually add the sugar and ground ginger, beating continuously until stiff peaks form. Fold in the grated fresh ginger. Spread some icing over the top of each cupcake. Dust with a little ground ginger and decorate with a slice of crystallized ginger. These cupcakes should be iced just before serving.

Persimmon Nut Treats

Makes 18

250g plain flour
2 teaspoons baking powder
1 teaspoon salt
1 teaspoon ground cinnamon
1/2 teaspoon ground ginger
Pinch each of freshly grated nutmeg
   and ground cloves
1 tablespoon finely grated orange zest
250g unsalted butter, softened
150g granulated sugar
150g soft light brown sugar
1 egg, lightly beaten
200g puréed persimmon pulp (about
   3 very ripe persimmons)
200g nuts, such as walnuts, pecan nuts
   or hazelnuts, coarsely ground

For the icing
240g cream cheese or full-fat
   soft cheese, softened
30g unsalted butter, softened
225g icing sugar, sifted
1 teaspoon finely grated orange zest
2 teaspoons freshly squeezed orange
   juice

Dried persimmons, to decorate

1 Preheat the oven to 180°C/350°F/Gas mark 4. Grease 18 cups of two 12-cup tins or line 18 cups with paper cupcake cases. For the cupcakes, sift all the dry ingredients into a bowl, then stir in the orange zest. Set aside.

2 Cream the butter and sugars together in a separate large bowl until pale and fluffy. Add the egg and beat well. Alternately add the flour mixture and persimmon pulp to the creamed mixture, beating well after each addition. Fold in the nuts.

3 Spoon the batter into the prepared cupcake cups, filling each cup about two-thirds full. Smooth the tops. Bake in the oven for 25 minutes, or until a skewer inserted into the centre comes out clean. Remove from the oven and leave to cool completely before turning out.

4 To make the icing, beat the cream cheese or soft cheese and butter together in a bowl until smooth. Gradually add the icing sugar and beat until pale and fluffy. Beat in the orange zest and juice. Cover and refrigerate for 1 hour. Spread the top of each cupcake with some icing and decorate each one with a piece of dried persimmon.

Strawberry Rhubarb
Crisp Cupcakes

Makes 16

150g rhubarb (fresh or frozen),
  chopped
200g caster sugar, plus 3 tablespoons
  if you are using fresh rhubarb (see
  Step 1)
200g plain flour
2 teaspoons baking powder
1 teaspoon bicarbonate of soda
1 teaspoon salt
1 teaspoon ground cinnamon
125g unsalted butter, softened
2 eggs, lightly beaten
1 teaspoon vanilla extract
250ml buttermilk
115g strawberry jam
175g fresh strawberries, cut into
  quarters lengthways, to decorate

1 If you are using fresh rhubarb, wash and peel the rhubarb, cut it into small slices (as you would celery) and place it in a colander in the sink or over a bowl. Sprinkle with the 3 tablespoons of sugar and leave to drain for 30 minutes. This will make the rhubarb more tender and will bring out its taste.

2 Preheat the oven to 180°C/350°F/Gas mark 4. Grease 16 cups of two 12-cup tins or regular silicone cupcake moulds, or line 16 cups with paper cupcake or muffin cases. Sift the flour, baking powder, bicarbonate of soda, salt and cinnamon into a bowl and set aside.

3 Cream the butter and the 200g of sugar together in a separate large bowl until pale and fluffy. Gradually add the eggs, beating well after each addition. Add the vanilla extract. Alternately add the flour mixture and buttermilk to the creamed mixture, beating continuously. When the batter is smooth, fold in the prepared fresh or frozen rhubarb.

4 Spoon the batter into the prepared cupcake cups, filling each cup about two-thirds full. Bake in the oven for 20–25 minutes, or until a skewer inserted into the centre comes out clean. Turn out onto a wire rack and leave to cool.

5 Heat the jam in a small saucepan over a very low heat until just melted. Remove the pan from the heat and brush some of the jam over the cupcakes using a pastry brush. Place strawberry quarters in a circle in the centre of each cupcake, then brush with a little jam.

S'mores Cupcakes

Makes 18

75g plain flour
175g digestive biscuits (about
    20 biscuits), finely crushed
2 teaspoons baking powder
1 teaspoon salt
125g unsalted butter,
150g caster sugar
2 eggs, lightly beaten
1 teaspoon vanilla extract
175ml milk
125g milk chocolate chips

For the icing
2 egg whites
Pinch of salt or cream of tartar
50g caster sugar
175ml golden syrup

**Grated milk chocolate or chocolate
    sprinkles, to decorate**

1 Preheat the oven to 180°C/350°F/Gas mark 4.
Grease 18 cups of two 12-cup tins or line
18 cups with paper cupcake cases. For the
cupcakes, mix the flour, biscuit crumbs, baking
powder and salt together in a bowl and set aside.

2 Cream the butter and sugar together in a
separate bowl until pale and fluffy. Gradually
add the eggs, beating well after each addition. Add
the vanilla extract. Alternately add the flour mixture
and milk to the creamed mixture and beat until the
batter is smooth. Fold in the chocolate chips.

3 Spoon the batter into the prepared cupcake
cups, filling each cup about two-thirds full.
Bake in the oven for 20–25 minutes, or until a
skewer inserted into the centre comes out clean.
Turn out onto a wire rack and leave to cool.

4 For the icing, whisk the egg whites with the
salt or cream of tartar in a bowl until soft peaks
form. Gradually add the sugar, whisking
continuously. Slowly add the golden syrup, whisking
until the icing forms peaks and has a marshmallow
consistency. Spread the top of each cupcake with
some icing. Sprinkle with grated chocolate or
chocolate sprinkles to decorate. Leave to set
before serving.

Birthday Beauties

Makes 12

375g plain flour
150g caster sugar
2½ teaspoons baking powder
1 teaspoon bicarbonate of soda
½ teaspoon salt
250ml buttermilk
185g unsalted butter, melted
2 eggs, lightly beaten
1 teaspoon vanilla extract
175g fresh strawberries, cut into small
   pieces

For the icing
About 250g glacé icing or ready-made
   vanilla butter cream icing
Food colouring (various colours)

To decorate
Desiccated coconut
Chocolate sprinkles
Sweets
Coloured sugars
Crystallized fruits
Nuts

1 Preheat the oven to 180°C/350°F/Gas mark 4. Grease a 12-cup tin or line the cups with paper cupcake cases. For the cupcakes, mix the flour, sugar, baking powder, bicarbonate of soda and salt together in a large bowl and set aside.

2 In a separate bowl, mix the buttermilk, melted butter, eggs and vanilla extract together. Add the wet ingredients to the flour mixture and beat well with a wooden spoon until thoroughly mixed. Fold in the strawberries.

3 Spoon the batter into the prepared cupcake cups, filling each cup about two-thirds full. Bake in the oven for 20–25 minutes, or until a skewer inserted into the centre comes out clean. Turn out onto a wire rack and leave to cool.

4 For the icing, divide the glacé or butter cream icing into portions (depending on how many different colours of icing you require) and put each portion into a separate bowl. Add several drops of food colouring to each bowl, blending it in until you obtain the desired colour. Top each cupcake with some of the icing and decorate with desiccated coconut, chocolate sprinkles, sweets, coloured sugars, crystallized fruit and nuts, and leave to set, if necessary, before serving.

Lemon Meringue Cupcakes

Makes 12

225g plain flour
2 teaspoons baking powder
1 teaspoon salt
2 tablespoons finely grated lemon zest
125g unsalted butter, softened
200g caster sugar
2 eggs, lightly beaten
2 tablespoons freshly squeezed lemon
   juice

For the lemon cream

150g caster sugar
3 tablespoons plain flour
Pinch of salt
4 tablespoons freshly squeezed lemon
   juice
Finely grated zest of 1 lemon
3 egg yolks, beaten
65g unsalted butter, cut into small
   pieces

For the meringue

3 egg whites
Pinch of salt
50g caster sugar, plus extra for dusting
A few teaspoons of icing or caster
   sugar, for dusting

1 For the lemon cream, mix the sugar, flour and salt together in a large heat-proof bowl. Add the lemon juice and zest and mix well. Beat in 125ml of water, the egg yolks and butter. Set over a pan of barely simmering water. Cook until smooth and thick, stirring continuously with a whisk – about 20 minutes. Remove from the heat and set aside to cool.

2 Preheat the oven to 180°C/350°F/Gas mark 4. Grease a 12-cup tin or line with paper cupcake cases. For the cupcakes, mix the flour, baking powder, salt and lemon zest together in a bowl. Cream the butter and sugar together in a separate bowl until pale and fluffy. Gradually add the eggs, beating well after each addition. Add the lemon juice and beat well. Add the flour mixture and beat until smooth.

3 Spoon the batter into the prepared cupcake cups, dividing it evenly. Bake for 15 minutes, or until golden. Cool in the tin for 10 minutes. Meanwhile, for the meringue, whisk the egg whites with the salt until they start to stiffen. Gradually add the sugar. Whisk until stiff but not dry.

4 Using a sharp knife, remove a cone from the centre of each cupcake. Fill with the lemon cream. Top each cupcake with 1 tablespoon of the meringue, forming peaks with a fork. Dust with caster sugar. Bake for 5–7 minutes, or until just golden. Leave to cool before turning out.

Hot Chocolate &
Marshmallow Cupcakes

Makes 12

240g plain chocolate, broken into
    squares
250g unsalted butter,
4 eggs
200g caster sugar
125g plain flour
1 teaspoon salt
60g chocolate chips or grated plain
    chocolate
Large marshmallows or mini
    marshmallows, to decorate

1 Preheat the oven to 180°C/350°F/Gas mark 4. Grease a 12-cup tin or line the cups with paper cupcake cases. Put the chocolate and butter in a large heat-proof bowl set over a pan of barely simmering water and heat until just melted and combined. Remove the bowl from the heat and set aside until just warm.

2 Whisk the eggs and sugar together in a separate bowl until pale and foamy. Add the flour and salt and whisk to mix. Pour in the melted chocolate mixture and whisk until the batter is smooth and well mixed.

3 Spoon the batter into the prepared cupcake cups, dividing it evenly. Sprinkle a teaspoon of chocolate chips or grated chocolate over each cupcake. Bake in the oven for 15 minutes, then remove the cupcakes from oven – they will be very moist inside at this stage.

4 Meanwhile, preheat the grill to medium-high. Place a large marshmallow or several mini marshmallows on top of each cupcake. Put the cupcakes under the grill for a few seconds only until the marshmallows start to brown.

5 Remove the cupcakes from the grill and transfer them to a wire rack. Leave for about 5 minutes before turning out and eating the cupcakes, as the marshmallows will be very hot. These cupcakes are best eaten while still slightly warm.

Brownie Cupcakes

Makes 12

150g plain flour
1 teaspoon baking powder
1 teaspoon salt
180g plain chocolate, broken into
    squares
80g unsalted butter, cut into small
    pieces
150g caster sugar
2 eggs, lightly beaten
1 teaspoon vanilla extract
100g walnuts, chopped

For the icing
90g plain chocolate, roughly chopped
200g caster sugar
5 tablespoons milk
40g unsalted butter, cut into small
    pieces
1 tablespoon golden syrup
Pinch of salt
1 teaspoon vanilla extract
50g walnuts, chopped (optional)
12 walnut halves and 12 chocolate
    buttons, to decorate

1 Preheat the oven to 180°C/350°F/Gas mark 4. Grease a 12-cup tin or line the cups with paper cupcake cases. For the cupcakes, sift the flour, baking powder and salt into a bowl and set aside.

2 Melt the chocolate, butter and sugar in a large heat-proof bowl set over a pan of barely simmering water, stirring occasionally. Remove the bowl from the heat, then gradually add the eggs, beating well after each addition. Add the vanilla extract. Gradually add the flour mixture to the chocolate mixture, beating well until smooth, then fold in the walnuts.

3 Spoon the batter into the prepared cupcake cups, dividing it evenly. Smooth the tops. Bake for about 20–25 minutes or until crusty but a little moist inside. Leave to cool completely before removing and turning out.

4 Put all the icing ingredients, except the vanilla extract and walnuts, in a heavy-based saucepan. Bring to the boil and cook for 1 minute, stirring continuously. Remove from the heat and cool.

5 Add the vanilla extract to the icing and beat the mixture for about 10 minutes, or until thick and fluffy and the colour has slightly lightened. If you are using chopped walnuts, fold them in now. Spread the icing over the tops of the cupcakes. Top each cupcake with a walnut half and a chocolate button to decorate.

Rum Raisin Cupcakes

with Butter Rum Icing

Makes 16 regular or 40 mini cupcakes

100g raisins, plus extra to decorate
4 tablespoons dark rum
185g plain flour
1½ teaspoons baking powder
1 teaspoon salt
150g unsalted butter, cut into small
  pieces
150g soft light brown sugar
3 eggs, lightly beaten

For the icing
60g unsalted butter, softened
300g icing sugar, sifted
Pinch of salt

1 For the cupcakes, soak the raisins in the rum in a small bowl for about 30 minutes, stirring occasionally. Drain the raisins, reserving the rum for the icing, and set aside.

2 Preheat the oven to 180°C/350°F/Gas mark 4. Grease 16 cups of two 12-cup tins or regular silicone cupcake moulds, or grease 40 cups of two 24-cup mini muffin tins or mini silicone cupcake moulds, or line 16 or 40 cups with paper cupcake or mini muffin cases. Sift the flour, baking powder and salt into a bowl and set aside.

3 Melt the butter and sugar together in a small saucepan over a low heat, stirring continuously. When the sugar has dissolved, remove the pan from the heat, pour the mixture into a well in the centre of the flour mixture and mix well. Add the drained raisins and the eggs and stir vigorously with a wooden spoon until the batter is smooth.

4 Spoon the batter into the prepared cupcake cups, filling each cup about two-thirds full. Bake in the oven for about 25 minutes, or until a skewer inserted into the centre comes out clean. Turn out onto a wire rack and leave to cool.

5 For the icing, cream the butter, sugar and salt together in a bowl until pale and fluffy. Beat in the reserved rum. If the icing is too thick, add more rum; if too thin, add more sugar. Spread over the tops of the cupcakes and decorate with raisins.

Boston Cream Cupcakes

Makes 18

300g plain flour
2 teaspoons baking powder
1 teaspoon salt
125g unsalted butter, softened
200g caster sugar
3 egg yolks, beaten
175ml milk
1 teaspoon vanilla extract

For the filling
350ml milk
1 vanilla pod or 1 teaspoon vanilla
   extract
100g caster sugar
35g plain flour
2 eggs, plus 2 egg yolks
Chocolate Ganache (page 115),
   to decorate

1 Preheat the oven to 180°C/350°F/Gas mark 4. Grease 18 cups of two 12-cup tins or regular silicone cupcake moulds, or line 18 cups with paper cupcake or muffin cases. For the cupcakes, sift the flour, baking powder and salt into a bowl and set aside.

2 Cream the butter and sugar together in a separate bowl until pale and fluffy. Add the egg yolks all at once and beat well. Alternately beat in the flour mixture and milk, mixing well, then beat in the vanilla extract. Spoon the batter into the prepared cupcake cases, filling each cup about two-thirds full. Bake in the oven for 20–25 minutes, or until a skewer inserted into the centre comes out clean. Turn out onto a wire rack and leave to cool.

3 For the filling, heat the milk with the vanilla pod or vanilla extract in a small saucepan until it reaches boiling point, then remove the pan from the heat and set aside to cool slightly. Remove the vanilla pod, split lengthways and scrape out the seeds into the milk.

4 In a separate large heat-proof bowl, combine the sugar, flour, eggs and egg yolks and whisk together until pale and creamy. Set the bowl over a pan of barely simmering water, then slowly add the milk, stirring continuously, and cook until the mixture just starts to boil. Remove the bowl from the heat and continue stirring for a few minutes. Leave to cool before using.

5 Cut the cupcakes in half and fill with the custard filling. Ice the tops of the cupcakes with the chocolate ganache.

Bourdaloue Cupcakes
with Caramelized Almonds

Makes 6–8 jumbo cupcakes

185g unsalted butter, softened
100g caster sugar
3 eggs, lightly beaten
2 teaspoons vanilla extract
185g ground almonds
35g plain flour
1 teaspoon salt
6–8 pear halves (fresh or canned), cut
   lengthways into quarters

For the caramelized almonds
100g flaked almonds
50g granulated sugar

1 Preheat the oven to 180°C/350°F/Gas mark 4. Grease 6-8 cups of a 12-cup muffin tin or jumbo silicone cupcake mould, or line 6–8 cups with paper muffin or jumbo cupcake cases.

2 For the cupcakes, cream the butter and sugar together in a bowl until pale and fluffy. Gradually add the eggs, beating well after each addition. Add the vanilla extract, the ground almonds, flour and salt and beat until smooth.

3 Spoon the batter into the prepared cupcake cups, dividing it evenly. Place two pear quarters in the top of each cupcake, pressing them in lightly. Bake in the oven for 30 minutes, or until golden brown and the tops spring back when lightly pressed. Remove from the oven and leave to cool completely before turning out.

4 For the caramelized almonds, mix the almonds and sugar together in a cold non-stick saucepan. Turn the heat to high, stirring continuously. When the almonds start to brown (this will take only a few minutes), remove the pan from the heat and pour the almonds immediately into a heat-proof dish, then set aside to cool completely. Gently break them loose with a fork or your fingers. Sprinkle the caramelized almonds over the cupcakes just before serving.

Tip
Bake these in a silicone mould and serve with Créme Anglaise (see page 97).

Chocolate Charlotte
Cupcakes

Makes 8–10 jumbo cupcakes

240g plain chocolate, broken into
    squares
125g unsalted butter, cut into small
    pieces
100g caster sugar
3 eggs, separated
125ml whipping cream
Pinch of salt
1 packet of sponge fingers
Unsweetened orange juice, for soaking
Crème Anglaise (page 97), to serve

1 Grease 8–10 cups of a 12-cup tin or jumbo silicone cupcake mould. Melt the chocolate, butter and sugar together in a heat-proof bowl set over a pan of barely simmering water, stirring occasionally.

2 Remove the bowl from the heat, then add the egg yolks to the melted mixture, one at a time, beating well after each addition. Leave to cool, then pour in the cream and stir to mix – the mixture will thicken.

3 Whisk the egg whites with the salt in a separate bowl until stiff but not dry. Gently fold the whisked egg whites into the chocolate mixture.

4 To assemble the cupcakes, briefly dip the sponge fingers in the orange juice – you don't want them to be soggy. Use to line the sides of the prepared muffin or silicone cupcake cups, cutting the sponge fingers to size and squeezing them together tightly. Fill the lined cups with the chocolate mixture to just a little below the top, dividing it evenly. Cover the cupcakes with more sponge fingers dipped in orange juice, fitting them well to cover all the chocolate. Cover the cupcakes with cling film and chill in the refrigerator for several hours or overnight.

5 Unmould the cupcakes onto a serving dish and serve them upside-down, either in pretty paper muffin or jumbo cupcake cases or on a plate. Serve with the crème Anglaise.

Cevenol Cupcakes

Makes 16

100g plain flour
2 teaspoons baking powder
1 teaspoon salt
80g unsalted butter, softened
400g 'crème de marron' chestnut
  spread (can be found in most
  gourmet food shops or delicatessens)
100g caster sugar
2 eggs, lightly beaten
2 tablespoons dark rum
8 glazed chestnuts (can be found in
  most gourmet food shops or
  delicatessens), halved, to decorate

1 Preheat the oven to 180°C/350°F/Gas mark 4.
Grease 16 cups of two 12-cup tins or line
16 cups with paper cupcake cases.

2 Sift the flour, baking powder and salt into a
bowl and set aside. Cream the butter and 200g
of the chestnut spread together in a bowl until
smooth and creamy. Add the sugar, eggs and rum
and beat together until thoroughly mixed. Stir in
the flour mixture, mixing well.

3 Spoon the batter into the prepared cupcake
cups, filling each cup about two-thirds full.
Bake in the oven for about 25 minutes, or until a
skewer inserted into the centre comes out clean.
Turn out onto a wire rack and leave to cool
completely.

4 Spread the tops of the cupcakes with the
remaining chestnut spread, then top each one
with a glazed chestnut half.

Mendicant Cupcakes

Makes 16

75g blanched hazelnuts, roasted and
   roughly ground
75g blanched almonds, roasted and
   roughly ground
300g plain flour
2 teaspoons baking powder
1 teaspoon bicarbonate of soda
1 teaspoon salt
1 teaspoon ground cinnamon
$\frac{1}{2}$ teaspoon ground allspice
125g unsalted butter, softened
200g soft dark brown sugar
2 eggs, lightly beaten
4 teaspoons white wine vinegar
150ml milk
75g raisins

For the topping
400g dried figs
1 cinnamon stick
150g granulated sugar

1 For the cupcakes, sift the flour, baking powder,
bicarbonate of soda, salt and ground spices into a
bowl. Set aside. Cream the butter and sugar together
in a separate bowl until pale and fluffy. Gradually add
the eggs, beating well after each addition. Combine
the vinegar and milk in a small bowl. Alternately add
the flour mixture and milk mixture to the creamed
mixture, beating well after each addition until
smooth. Fold in the raisins and ground nuts

2 Preheat the oven to 180°C/350°F/Gas mark 4.
Grease 16 cups of two 12-cup tins or regular
silicone cupcake moulds, or line 16 cups with
paper cupcake or muffin cases.

3 Put all the topping ingredients in a heavy-based
saucepan together with 375ml of water and
bring to the boil. Reduce the heat and simmer for
about 20 minutes, or until the figs are tender and
about half of the water has evaporated. Remove the
pan from the heat, then remove and discard the
cinnamon stick. Process the fig mixture in a blender
or food processor until well blended. Set aside.

4 Spoon the batter into the cupcake cups, filling
each just a little over half full. Bake in the oven
for about 20 minutes, or until just barely cooked.

5 Remove from oven and spread some fig
mixture over the top of each cupcake. Return
the cupcakes to the oven and bake for a further
10 minutes, or until cooked. Remove from the oven
and leave the cupcakes to cool completely before
removing them from the tins or moulds.

Opera Cupcakes

Makes 12 regular or 6 jumbo cupcakes

65g unsalted butter, cut into small pieces
125g finely ground almonds
130g caster sugar, plus 2 tablespoons
35g plain flour
4 eggs, separated
Pinch of salt

Chocolate Ganache (page 115) made
using 125g chocolate and 125ml
double cream
Half a quantity of Mocha Butter Cream
Icing (page 234)
Edible gold leaf, to decorate

1 Preheat the oven to 120°C/250°F/Gas mark ½.
Grease a 12-cup tin or regular silicone cupcake
mould, or grease 6 cups of a 12-cup muffin tin or
jumbo silicone cupcake mould, or line 12 or 6 cups
with paper cupcake or muffin cases.

2 For the cupcakes, melt the butter in a small
saucepan, then remove the pan from the heat
and set aside until cool. Beat the ground almonds,
130g of sugar, the flour and egg yolks together in a
bowl until the mixture is pale and foamy

3 In a separate bowl, whisk the egg whites with
the salt and remaining sugar until the mixture
is stiff but not dry. Gently fold the whisked egg
whites into the almond mixture. Carefully add the
cooled butter mixture, using a spatula or a whisk
to mix.

4 Spoon the batter into the prepared cupcake
cups, filling each cup just a little over half full.
Bake in the oven for about 10 minutes, or until
brown on top. Be careful not to burn these
cupcakes – they will cook quickly. Remove from
the oven and leave to cool completely.

5 Turn the cupcakes out and cut each one into
three equal layers. Using a hand-held electric
mixer, beat half of the chocolate ganache in a bowl
for about 5–10 minutes, or until it is pale and fluffy.
If the other half hardens, set it over a pan of warm
water until the right consistency.

6 To assemble, spread some mocha butter cream
icing on the first layer of each cupcake. Add a
second layer of cupcake and spread some beaten
chocolate ganache over this layer. Add a third layer
of cupcake and ice with liquid chocolate ganache.
Decorate with a piece of edible gold leaf and serve
in pretty paper cupcake or muffin cases.

Far Breton Cupcakes

Makes 12

12 stoned dried prunes
1 small glass of rum (about
    4 tablespoons)
115g plain flour
Pinch of salt
100g caster sugar
2 eggs, lightly beaten
350ml milk
65g unsalted butter, melted and cooled
Sifted icing sugar, for dusting
Crème Anglaise (page 97), to serve

Tip
Alternatively, just serve these cupcakes in pretty cupcake papers dusted with sifted icing sugar.

1 Soak the prunes in the rum in a bowl for about 1 hour, stirring occasionally. Drain the prunes, reserving the rum, and save. Set the prunes aside.

2 Preheat the oven to 180°C/350°F/Gas mark 4. Grease a 12-cup tin or regular silicone cupcake mould. Mix the flour, salt and caster sugar together in a large bowl. In a separate bowl, beat the eggs with the milk and melted butter, then add this liquid to the flour mixture, mixing well with a wooden spoon or a hand-held electric mixer. The batter will be liquid. Stir in 2 tablespoons of the reserved rum.

3 Place a prune in each of the prepared cupcake cups. Spoon the batter into the cups, filling each cup about half full. Bake in the oven for about 35 minutes, or until brown on top. The batter will rise and then deflate when it cools. Cool in the tin or mould for 10–15 minutes, then turn out onto a wire rack and leave to cool completely.

4 Sprinkle each cupcake with sifted icing sugar and serve lukewarm on a plate with the crème Anglaise, to which you have added a little of the remaining reserved rum.

Irish Coffee Cupcakes

Makes 16

225g plain flour
150g soft light brown sugar
1 teaspoon baking powder
1 teaspoon bicarbonate of soda
1 teaspoon salt
1 teaspoon ground cinnamon
$\frac{1}{2}$ teaspoon ground ginger
Pinch of freshly grated nutmeg
100g raisins
65g nuts, such as pistachio nuts,
   walnuts or hazelnuts, coarsely
   chopped
2 eggs, lightly beaten
125ml vegetable oil
125ml Irish whiskey
4 tablespoons single cream or milk

For the mocha butter cream icing

250g unsalted butter, softened and cut
   into small pieces
250g icing sugar, sifted
2 egg yolks
1 tablespoon coffee extract or very
   strong brewed coffee (add more or
   less, depending on your taste)

1 Preheat the oven to 180°C/350°F/Gas mark 4. Grease 16 cups of two 12-cup tins or line 16 cups with paper cupcake cases.

2 For the cupcakes, mix all the dry ingredients together in a large bowl. Add the eggs, vegetable oil, whiskey and cream or milk and mix thoroughly with a wooden spoon until well combined.

3 Spoon the batter into the prepared cupcake cases, filling each cup about two-thirds full. Bake in the oven for 25–30 minutes, or until a skewer inserted into the centre comes out clean. Turn out onto a wire rack and leave to cool.

4 To make the icing, cream the butter and sugar together in a bowl until pale and fluffy. Add the egg yolks and coffee extract or brewed coffee to taste and beat until the mixture is light, shiny and of a good spreading consistency (this will take at least 10 minutes). Spread some icing over the top of each cupcake before serving.

Clafoutis with *Crème Anglaise*

Makes 16

75g ground almonds
185g plain flour
1½ teaspoons baking powder
1 teaspoon salt
125g unsalted butter, softened
200g caster sugar
2 eggs, lightly beaten
125ml milk
1 small shot glass of cherry brandy
  (optional)
250g stoned fresh or frozen cherries
  (if using frozen cherries, don't thaw)
maraschino cherries, to decorate

Crème Anglaise (page 97) cooled, to
serve

1 Preheat the oven to 180°C/350°F/Gas mark 4.
Grease 16 cups of two 12-cup tins or regular
silicone cupcake moulds, or line 16 cups with
paper cupcake or muffin cases.

2 For the cupcakes, mix the ground almonds,
flour, baking powder and salt together in a bowl
and set aside. Cream the butter and sugar together
in a separate bowl until pale and fluffy. Gradually
add the eggs, beating well after each addition.
Alternately beat in the flour mixture and milk,
mixing well. Add the cherry brandy, if using, and beat
the batter until smooth. Fold in the fresh cherries.

3 Spoon the batter into the prepared cupcake
cups, filling each cup about two-thirds full.
Bake in the oven for 20–25 minutes, or until a
skewer inserted into the centre comes out clean.
Remove from the oven and top each cupcake with
a maraschino cherry. Cool the cupcakes in the tin
or mould for 5 minutes, then turn out onto a wire
rack and leave to cool completely.

4 Serve the cupcakes with the cooled crème
anglaise in a jug or bowl.

Frozen Lemon Cupcakes

Makes 12

For the lemon cream
200g caster sugar
Finely grated zest and juice of 1 lemon
475ml whipping cream

For the biscuit base
125g unsalted butter, softened
75g digestive biscuits, crushed
75g cornflakes, crushed
2 tablespoons caster sugar
Jellied or crystallized lemon slices,
   to decorate

1 Grease a 12-cup tin or regular silicone cupcake mould. For the lemon cream, combine the sugar and lemon zest and juice in a large bowl. Gradually whisk in the cream. Set aside.

2 For the biscuit base, melt the butter in a small saucepan over a low heat. Remove the pan from the heat and stir in the biscuit crumbs, crushed cornflakes and sugar.

3 Press some of the biscuit base mixture into the base of each of the prepared cupcake cups, dividing it evenly. Pour some of the lemon cream mixture over each biscuit base, dividing it evenly. Cover with freezer wrap and freeze for at least 3 hours. Unmould the cupcakes, top each one with a jellied or crystallized lemon slice and serve.

Tip
You can use cupcake papers or make these frozen cupcakes in either a rigid or a silicone mould.

Mother's Day Rose
Cupcakes

Makes 18

400g plain flour
3 teaspoons baking powder
1 teaspoon salt
125g unsalted butter, softened
150g caster sugar
2 eggs, lightly beaten
4 tablespoons rose syrup
250ml milk
Rose jam (or strawberry or raspberry
  jam, if rose jam is not available)

For the icing
90g unsalted butter, softened
300g icing sugar, sifted
3 tablespoons rose syrup
$\frac{1}{2}$ teaspoon rosewater (optional)
Red food colouring (optional)
Decorations of your choice

1 Preheat the oven to 180°C/350°F/Gas mark 4. Grease 18 cups of two 12-cup tins or line 18 cups with paper cupcake cases.

2 For the cupcakes, sift the flour, baking powder and salt into a bowl and set aside. Cream the butter and sugar together in a separate bowl until pale and fluffy. Gradually add the eggs, beating well after each addition. Alternately add the flour mixture, rose syrup and milk to the creamed mixture, beating well after each addition.

3 Spoon the batter into the prepared cupcake cups, filling each cup about two-thirds full. Bake in the oven for 25–30 minutes, or until a skewer inserted into the centre comes out clean. Turn out onto a wire rack and leave to cool. Using a sharp knife, remove a cone from the centre of each cupcake. Drop a teaspoonful of rose jam into each and replace the cones.

4 For the icing, cream the butter and sugar together in a bowl until pale and fluffy. Gradually add the rose syrup, rosewater and food colouring, if using, beating continuously until a good spreading consistency. Spread over the tops of the cupcakes with some icing and decorate to your taste.

July 4th Blueberry
& Raspberry Cupcakes

Makes 12 regular or 6 jumbo cupcakes

250g plain flour
2 teaspoons baking powder
1 teaspoon bicarbonate of soda
1 teaspoon salt
125g unsalted butter, softened
130g caster sugar
1 egg, lightly beaten
250ml buttermilk
1 teaspoon vanilla extract
100g blueberries (fresh or frozen)
100g raspberries (fresh or frozen)
Sifted icing sugar, for dusting
115g raspberry jam
Extra raspberries and blueberries,
   to decorate

1 Preheat the oven to 180°C/350°F/Gas mark 4. Grease a 12-cup tin or regular silicone cupcake mould, or grease 6 cups of a 12-cup muffin tin or jumbo silicone cupcake mould, or line 12 or 6 cups with paper cupcake or muffin cases.

2 Sift the flour, baking powder, bicarbonate of soda and salt into a bowl and set aside. Cream the butter and caster sugar together in a separate bowl until pale and fluffy. Add the egg, buttermilk and vanilla extract and mix well. Stir in the flour mixture, then gently fold in the blueberries and raspberries. If you are using frozen berries, don't thaw before using.

3 Spoon the batter into the prepared cupcake cups, filling each cup about two-thirds full. Bake in the oven for about 25 minutes, or until golden brown. Remove from the oven and leave the cupcakes to cool completely before turning out. Dust the cupcakes with sifted icing sugar.

4 Heat the raspberry jam in a small saucepan over a very low heat until just melted, then remove the pan from the heat. Place a few raspberries in the centre on the top of each cupcake (preferably while the icing is still soft). Surround with blueberries. Using a pastry brush, brush the warm jam over the fruit.

Easter Lavender Cupcakes

Makes 24–30

200g plain flour
2 teaspoons baking powder
1 teaspoon salt
125g unsalted butter, softened
150g caster sugar
2 eggs, lightly beaten
1 teaspoon vanilla extract
125ml single cream
2 tablespoons dried lavender flowers
2 tablespoons poppy seeds, for
   sprinkling
Several teaspoons of your favourite
   jam, to decorate

For the filling

250ml whipping cream, chilled
4 tablespoons icing sugar, sifted
$\frac{1}{2}$ teaspoon lemon extract (or another
   flavouring of your choice)
1 tablespoon finely grated lemon zest
   (if using lemon extract)

1 Preheat the oven to 180°C/350°F/Gas mark 4. Grease 24–30 cups of two or three 12-cup tins or line 24–30 cups with paper cupcake cases.

2 For the cupcakes, sift the flour, baking powder and salt into a bowl and set aside. Cream the butter and sugar together in a separate bowl until light and fluffy. Gradually add the eggs, beating well after each addition, then beat in the vanilla extract. Alternately beat the flour mixture and cream into the creamed mixture, mixing well. Fold in the lavender flowers.

3 Spoon the batter into the prepared cupcake cups, filling each cup about two-thirds full. Bake in the oven for about 25 minutes, or until a skewer inserted into the centre comes out clean. Turn out onto a wire rack and leave to cool.

4 To make the filling, whip the cream in a large bowl. When it starts to thicken, gradually add the sugar and whip until stiff peaks form. Whisk in the lemon extract or other flavouring and lemon zest, if using.

5 Cut off the top of each cupcake and set aside – this will be the butterfly. Using a sharp knife, remove a cone from the centre of each cupcake and fill with whipped cream. Sprinkle with a few poppy seeds. Cut the top in half and place the halves on top of the cream to look like the wings of a butterfly. Put a little jam in between the two halves to look like the butterfly's body.

Apple Cider Cupcakes

Makes 12

225g plain flour
2 teaspoons baking powder
1 teaspoon salt
1 teaspoon ground cinnamon
125g unsalted butter, softened
130g caster sugar
2 eggs, lightly beaten
175ml sweet cider
150g ready-to-eat dried apple rings, cut
   into small pieces
Ground cinnamon, for dusting
Apple wedges (either dried or fresh)
   and walnut halves, to decorate

For the filling

3–4 medium cooking apples, peeled,
   cored and chopped into small pieces
200g soft light brown sugar
100g unsalted butter, cut into small
   pieces
1 teaspoon ground cinnamon
$^1/_2$ teaspoon salt

1 Preheat the oven to 180°C/350°F/Gas mark 4. Grease a 12-cup tin or line the cups with paper cupcake cases.

2 For the cupcakes, sift the flour, baking powder, salt and cinnamon into a bowl and set aside. Cream the butter and sugar together in a separate bowl until pale and fluffy. Gradually add the eggs, beating well after each addition. Alternately add the flour mixture and cider to the creamed mixture, beating until the batter is smooth and well combined. Fold in the dried apples.

3 Spoon the batter into the prepared cupcake cups, filling each cup about two-thirds full. Bake in the oven for about 25 minutes, or until a skewer inserted into the centre comes out clean. Turn out onto a wire rack and leave to cool.

4 Meanwhile, for the filling, combine all the ingredients together with 2 tablespoons of water in a heavy-based saucepan and cook over a low heat for about 5–10 minutes, or until the apples are soft. Remove the pan from the heat, crush the apples with a fork, and leave to cool. Using a sharp knife, remove a cone from the centre of each cupcake and fill with the apple filling.

5 Dust each cupcake with a little cinnamon and top with an apple wedge and walnut half before serving.

Halloween Orange Cupcakes

Makes 16

300g plain flour
2 teaspoons baking powder
1 teaspoon salt
125g unsalted butter
200g caster sugar
2 eggs, lightly beaten
Juice and finely grated zest of 1 orange
1 tablespoon freshly squeezed lemon
   juice
Few drops of orange food colouring

For the glaze
200g caster sugar
25g cornflour
250ml unsweetened orange juice
1 teaspoon freshly squeezed lemon juice
Pinch of salt
30g unsalted butter, cut into small pieces
A few drops of orange food colouring

1 Preheat the oven to 180°C/350°F/Gas mark 4. Grease 16 cups of two 12-cup tins or line 16 cups with paper cupcake cases.

2 For the cupcakes, sift the flour, baking powder and salt into a bowl and set aside. Cream the butter and sugar together in a separate bowl until light and fluffy. Gradually add the eggs, beating well after each addition.

3 Combine the orange and lemon juices in a measuring jug. Add enough cold water to make up to 150ml. Alternately add the flour mixture and fruit juice mixture to the creamed mixture. Add the orange zest and beat until the batter is smooth and well combined. Stir in the food colouring.

4 Spoon the batter into the prepared cupcake cups, filling each cup about two-thirds full. Bake in the oven for 25 minutes, or until a skewer inserted into the centre comes out clean. Turn out onto a wire rack and leave to cool.

5 To make the glaze, combine the sugar and cornflour in a saucepan and heat over a low heat. Gradually add the orange and lemon juices and stir until smooth and well combined. Add the salt and butter. Cook over a low heat, stirring continuously, until the mixture is thick and glossy. Remove the pan from the heat and set aside to cool. Stir in the food colouring.

6 Spread some of the cooled orange glaze over the top of each cupcake.

Mezzo-Mezzo Cupcakes

Makes 16 regular, 8 jumbo or 40 mini cupcakes

200g plain flour
2 teaspoons baking powder
1 teaspoon bicarbonate of soda
1 teaspoon salt
75g unsweetened cocoa powder
200g soft light brown sugar
3 tablespoons instant cappuccino
   powder
125g unsalted butter, melted
2 eggs, lightly beaten
250ml soured cream

For the icing

250ml whipping cream, chilled
3 tablespoons icing sugar, sifted
1 tablespoon unsweetened cocoa
   powder, plus extra for dusting
1 tablespoon instant cappuccino
   powder
Chocolate coffee beans, to decorate

1 Preheat the oven to 180°C/350°F/Gas mark 4.
Grease 16 cups of two 12-cup tins or regular
silicone cupcake moulds, or grease 8 cups of a 12-cup
muffin tin or jumbo silicone cupcake mould, or

grease 40 cups of two 24-cup mini muffin tins or mini
silicone cupcake moulds, or line 16, 8 or 40 cups
with paper cupcake, muffin or mini muffin cases.

2 For the cupcakes, mix all the dry ingredients
together in a large bowl and set aside. Beat the
melted butter, eggs and soured cream together in a
separate bowl. Pour the butter mixture into the dry
ingredients, mixing rapidly with a wooden spoon
until the batter is smooth and well combined.

3 Spoon the batter into the prepared cupcake
cups, filling each cup about two-thirds full.
Bake in the oven for 15–20 minutes, or until a
skewer inserted into the centre comes out clean.
Turn out onto a wire rack and leave to cool.

4 To make the icing, put the cream, sugar, cocoa
powder and coffee powder in a large bowl. Stir
to mix, then cover and chill in the refrigerator for
about 1 hour, or until the cocoa and coffee have
dissolved. Remove from the refrigerator and beat
with a hand-held electric mixer until stiff.

5 Spread or pipe the chocolate icing over the
tops of the cooled cupcakes just before
serving. Dust with sifted cocoa powder and top
each cupcake with a chocolate coffee bean.

Christmas Fruit Cupcakes

Makes 12

200g assorted crystallized fruit,
roughly chopped
5 tablespoons brandy
300g plain flour
150g soft light brown sugar
2 teaspoons baking powder
1 teaspoon salt
1 teaspoon ground allspice
1 teaspoon ground cinnamon
½ teaspoon ground ginger
½ teaspoon freshly grated nutmeg
125ml milk
1 egg, lightly beaten
2 tablespoons apricot jam
1 teaspoon finely grated orange zest
1 teaspoon finely grated lemon zest
125g unsalted butter, melted

For the icing
150g icing sugar, sifted
1 teaspoon finely grated lemon zest
1 tablespoon freshly squeezed lemon
    juice
Decorations of your choice

1 Soak the crystallized fruits in the brandy in a bowl for 2 hours, stirring occasionally.

2 Preheat the oven to 180°C/350°F/Gas mark 4. Grease a 12-cup tin or regular silicone cupcake mould or line 12 cups with paper cupcake cases.

3 Mix the flour, sugar, baking powder, salt and spices together in a separate large bowl and set aside. In another bowl, lightly beat the milk with the egg, apricot jam, orange and lemon zests and melted butter. Add this to the flour mixture and mix well. Stir in the soaked fruit and brandy.

4 Spoon the batter into the prepared cupcake cups, filling each cup about two-thirds full. Bake in the oven for 20–30 minutes, or until a skewer inserted into the centre comes out clean. Turn out onto a wire rack and leave to cool.

5 To make the icing, mix the icing sugar and lemon zest together in a bowl, then gradually add enough of the lemon juice to make a smooth, spreadable icing paste. Spread some icing over the top of each cupcake and decorate to your taste. Leave to set before serving.

New Year's Eve Confetti
Cupcakes

Makes 12

150g plain flour
1 teaspoon baking powder
1 teaspoon salt
100g unsalted butter, cut into small
    pieces
100g caster sugar
3 eggs, lightly beaten
1 tablespoon brandy
5 tablespoons single cream
35g mints or hard sweets of different
    colours, crushed

For the icing
1 egg white
150g caster sugar
Pinch of salt
1 teaspoon golden syrup
1 tablespoon brandy
Confetti sprinkles, to decorate

1 Preheat the oven to 180°C/350°F/Gas mark 4. Grease a 12-cup tin or regular silicone cupcake mould, or line 12 with paper cupcake or mini muffin cases.

2 For the cupcakes, sift the flour, baking powder and salt into a bowl and set aside. Cream the butter and sugar together in a separate bowl until pale and fluffy. Gradually add the eggs, beating well after each addition, then beat in the brandy. Alternately beat the flour mixture and cream into the creamed mixture. Fold in the sweets.

3 Spoon the batter into the prepared cupcake cups, filling each cup about two-thirds full. Bake in the oven for about 20 minutes, or until a skewer inserted into the centre comes out clean. Turn out onto a wire rack and leave to cool.

4 For the icing, mix the egg white, sugar, salt, 3 tablespoons of water and golden syrup together in a heat-proof bowl. Place the bowl over a pan of barely simmering water and whisk until stiff peaks form.

5 Remove from the heat and transfer the mixture to another large bowl. Add the brandy and beat for a further 1 minute, or until spreadable. Spread over the tops of the cupcakes and sprinkle confetti sweets over each before the icing sets.

Pastis Cupcakes
with Anise Frosting

Makes 18

200g plain flour
2 teaspoons baking powder
1 teaspoon salt
180g unsalted butter, softened
150g caster sugar
3 eggs, lightly beaten
4 tablespoons pastis

For the icing
240g unsalted butter, softened and cut
    into small pieces
250g icing sugar, sifted
Pinch of salt
2 tablespoons pastis
Liquorice strands, liquorice sweets or
    black decorator icing, to decorate

1 Preheat the oven to 180°C/350°F/Gas mark 4.
  Grease 18 cups of two 12-cup tins or line
18 cups with paper cupcake cases.

2 For the cupcakes, sift the flour, baking powder
  and salt into a bowl and set aside. Cream the
butter and sugar together in a separate bowl until

pale and fluffy. Gradually add the eggs, beating well
after each addition. Alternately beat the flour
mixture and pastis into the creamed mixture,
mixing well.

3 Spoon the batter into the prepared cupcake
  cups, filling each cup about two-thirds full.
Bake in the oven for 25 minutes, or until a skewer
inserted into the centre comes out clean. Turn out
onto a wire rack and leave to cool.

4 For the icing beat the butter, sugar and salt
  together in a large bowl until pale and fluffy.
Add the pastis and continue to beat until the
mixture is of a good spreading consistency. Spread
the icing over the tops of the cupcakes. Decorate
each with a strand of liquorice, liquorice sweets or
black decorator icing.

Tip
If you prefer, use anise
syrup or liquorice
essence for a non-
alcoholic version.

Kir Cupcakes

Makes 20

250g plain flour
250g caster sugar
2 teaspoons baking powder
½ teaspoon salt, plus a pinch for the
   egg whites
125ml vegetable oil
125ml white wine
4 eggs, separated
150g currants

For the glaze
150g blackcurrant jam (about 8 heaped
   tablespoons)
2 tablespoons blackcurrant liqueur
   (optional)

To decorate
White decorator icing
Small sprigs of fresh or frozen
   redcurrants or blackcurrants, thawed
   if frozen (optional)

1 Preheat the oven to 180°C/350°F/Gas mark 4. Grease 20 cups of two 12-cup tins or line 20 cups with paper cupcake cases.

2 For the cupcakes, mix the flour, sugar, baking powder and salt together in a bowl. Gradually add the vegetable oil and wine, mixing well. Add the egg yolks, one at a time, beating well after each addition. The batter should be smooth and light. Set aside.

3 Whisk the egg whites with a pinch of salt in a separate bowl until stiff but not dry. Gently fold the whisked egg whites into the batter, then carefully fold in the currants.

4 Spoon the batter into the prepared cupcake cups, filling each cup about three-quarters full. Bake in the oven for about 20 minutes, or until a skewer inserted into the centre comes out clean. Turn out onto a wire rack and leave to cool.

5 To make the glaze, heat the blackcurrant jam in a small saucepan with the liqueur, if using, and cook for about 2 minutes. With a pastry brush, brush some of the glaze over each cupcake.

6 Set aside to allow the glaze to cool, then decorate each cupcake with a zig-zag of white decorator icing and small sprigs of redcurrants or blackcurrants, if you prefer.

After-Eight Cupcakes

Makes 12

200g plain flour
50g unsweetened cocoa powder
2 teaspoons baking powder
1 teaspoon salt
90g unsalted butter, softened
100g caster sugar
2 eggs, lightly beaten
150ml single cream
Few drops of peppermint essence
60g miniature chocolate mint chips
Double quantity of Chocolate Ganache
    (page 113)
12 chocolate-covered mint chocolates,
    to decorate (optional)

For the icing
185g unsalted butter, softened
300g icing sugar, sifted
2 tablespoons milk
Few drops of peppermint extract
Food colouring (optional)

1 Preheat the oven to 180°C/350°F/Gas mark 4. Grease a 12-cup tin or line the cups with paper cupcake cases.

2 For the cupcakes, sift the flour, cocoa powder, baking powder and salt into a bowl and set aside. Cream the butter and sugar together in a separate bowl until pale and fluffy. Gradually add the eggs, beating well after each addition. Alternately beat the flour mixture and cream into the creamed mixture. Add the peppermint essence and mix well.

3 Spoon the batter into the prepared cupcake cups, dividing it evenly. Sprinkle chocolate mint chips over the tops of the cupcakes, then bake in the oven for 20–25 minutes, or until a skewer inserted into the centre comes out clean. Turn out onto a wire rack and leave to cool.

4 To make the icing, cream the butter and sugar together in a bowl until pale and fluffy. Add the milk and peppermint essence and mix well. Add the food colouring if using. Spread the icing over the tops of the cupcakes, then leave to set.

5 Dip the cupcakes in the chocolate ganache, leaving a little of the butter cream icing showing around the edges. Place a chocolate-covered mint chocolate on top of each cupcake to decorate, if you like.

Index